Thommo

Thommo

JEFF THOMSON, the world's fastest bowler,
tells his own story to

DAVID FRITH

Foreword by DENNIS LILLEE

ANGUS & ROBERTSON PUBLISHERS

ANGUS & ROBERTSON PUBLISHERS
London • Sydney • Melbourne • Singapore • Manila

First published by Angus & Robertson Publishers,
Australia, 1980
Reprinted 1980

© Global Sportsman Pty Ltd, 1980

National Library of Australia
Cataloguing-in-publication data.

Frith, David, 1937 —
    Thommo.

    ISBN 0 207 14034 0

    1. Thomson, Jeff. 2. Cricket players —
Biography. I. Thomson, Jeff, joint author.
II. Title.

796.358'0924

Printed in Hong Kong

Contents

PHOTOGRAPHS

Between pages 72 and 73

Acknowledgements

Grateful thanks are due to Patrick Eagar for his jacket photographs and also for the following used in the book: 3, 4, 5, 6, 7, 8, 9, 10, 11, 12, 13, 14, 15, 16, 17, 19, 20, 21, 26. Thanks also to *Australian Cricket Magazine* for numbers 18 and 25; to Bob Thomas for 24, 28 and 30; and to Max Walker (the cricketer) for 22 and 23. All other photographs are from the Thomson family album.

Foreword
by Dennis Lillee

Many, many times I have been asked to give my thoughts on just what it is like to bowl at the other end to Jeff Thomson.

I can say in all honesty the experience has been the most fulfilling part of my cricket career so far. Apart from the sheer exhilaration of partnering such a great bowler, there are very real benefits — batsmen are so glad to get away from Thommo that sometimes they become easier pickings.

I am not sure what Thommo thinks about the subject, but I do know that when we are both firing together I feel a warm confidence against all·comers.

When I think about Thommo the bowler I get an immediate picture of absolutely frightening speed. And that always throws my mind back to what I believe was his greatest year — his real introduction to Test cricket against England in 1974-75, when I believe I saw all of their batsmen getting out through fright more than anything else.

Since that series obviously his fast bowling has been refined dramatically from brute force, without losing much in the way of pace or lift. Now he is a more complete bowler, while still retaining the crown as the fastest bowler in the world. You can throw in all your other quicks around the world, including Andy Roberts, Michael Holding, Wayne Daniel and Imran Khan, but there is no doubting Thommo has that extra edge in pace.

Over the years we have been together, the most striking thing that has hit me about Thommo is that I have hardly ever seen him blow up against a batsman. He seems to possess an extraordinary inner confidence in his own ability and takes the attitude, 'Oh well, he got away with it that time, but I'll get him soon enough.' Thommo is a really relaxed fellow, both on and off the field. And he's an easy guy to make friends with, as I have found along with many others over the years.

If you weigh up the contribution Thommo has made to the rebirth of cricket in Australia in the 1970s, you realise in a hurry what an enormous impact he has had on the sport in this country. He soon reached superstar status and, when people look back on the history of our wonderful game, they will record Thommo's name along with the greats in fast bowling.

But his contribution hasn't stopped at that point. He has in his own way revolutionised fast bowling through the development and perfection of his own slingshot style of delivery, a most effective method for the right physical specimen. This style has captured the imagination of a million cricket followers, and literally thousands of youngsters who have explored it thoroughly are bobbing up in junior cricket bowling 'Thommo style'. The sheer economy of this patented method of delivery could carry Thommo through many more seasons at the top, should that be his wish . . . I for one hope it is.

Introduction
by David Frith

I first laid eyes on Jeffrey Robert Thomson at a reception to the 1975 Australian touring team at Australia House, London. There he was, in the corner of the room, tall and clean-cut, wearing a caramel-coloured suit, gazing towards the chandeliers, sucking his teeth, obviously as bored as a rock'n'roller at a string quartet recital. The dark-suited gentlemen gathered around him put their mainly banal questions, and sometimes got a 'Yeah' by way of response. I think it was his mate and comrade-in-homicide, Dennis Lillee, who rescued him, and he was more at home with his mates. They formed a kind of pack, a protective formation, tribal, defiant, very self-satisfied.

He has seen a fair bit of the world since then, but has changed little. Less hesitant in a gathering, certainly, and not the complete reprobate. Certain responsibilities have come his way, some to stay, others short-lived. In the mid-seventies he was busy not only mowing down Poms but mowing down females as well. Melbourne *Truth* in February 1975 rated him cricket's Alvin Purple, quoting him as saying: 'When we go on tour we usually have a few beers at night and I often get hold of a bird or two. I choose the good-looking ones.' The only single man in the Australian side at that time, he was able to claim: 'I've taken out some real dolls, like beach beauties and models. They're the best.'

Now all that has changed. He married one of those pretty models, Cheryl Wilson, on December 18, 1976, at Holy Trinity Church, Valley, Brisbane. He couldn't recall the church, but said it was opposite Valley Police Station. The great fast bowler of earlier days, Ray Lindwall, now a Brisbane florist, supplied some of the flowers.

Earlier that same year Thommo was being put across as the playboy of the cricket world. Whichever ghost-writer of his it was saw fit to have him saying: 'I don't try to be Joe Blow the superstud — it just happens. But I don't let it get the better of me and reach the stage where my bowling is affected. No sir, everything in order.'

His name was once linked with the daughter of a prominent Australian politician, which tensed him up somewhat when he found out. And in England he was once the target not only for countless approaches by girls, but by a lady journalist who concealed her profession and intentions if little else. The team closed ranks, pooling their intelligence to prevent such infiltration.

Still they came, 'all shapes and sizes with just one thing in common — they wanted my body'. He was engaged twice (his devotion to cricket broke the second engagement) and in 1976 he was expecting an English lass to join him in Australia. Of all things, she had been studying Law at Oxford.

Everywhere he toured, letters from women admirers awaited him at the hotel reception desks, and the phone soon began ringing. He was a bachelor, utterly carefree. He took advantage of it all. It did not endear him to many people, some of whom thought it in very bad taste, especially when it was written up, and some of whom choked on their envy.

Then there was the homesickness on that first tour. Articles under his name appeared during the tour of England in 1975, and brought a risk of his being sent home. Fred Bennett, the manager, had to spell it out for him. Ian Chappell, toughest and most forthright of captains, threatened that if Thommo was told to pack his bags and go home, he would do so too. It died the death. As, eventually, did the homesickness.

While it lasted it was devastating. He missed his folks, and rang them frequently, at great expense. 'I can't lose myself over here,' he told his 'manager', David Lord, 'except for the odd game of golf, and that's not sufficient.' He was no longer the life of the party. He drooped. And, of course, his bowling suffered.

All fast bowlers — indeed, almost all bowlers generally — depend on rhythm. That rhythm can be disturbed by physical or mental factors. When Jeff Thomson's rhythm is right, and he is free of broken bones in the foot and torn shoulders, he is the fastest bowler in the world. Not the most verbal, not the one with the most intimidating run-up and hostile followthrough, but the one who leaves the batsman least time to sight the blurred, oncoming ball and do something about repelling it or dodging it.

This has always been the most captivating thing about Thommo. His attitude to sport is honest. He wants to be best and to win. He likes to laugh. He doesn't believe in backbiting — though when stung he can be unforgiving. He is even slightly old-fashioned in some of his attitudes and some of his expressions. This springs from being a home-loving boy with uncomplicated, caring, loving parents and three elder brothers and one younger. He is not ambitious, except to escape life's economic pressures. He loves the sea and the open land, and can admire a cloud formation with schoolboy wonder. But above all, he has brought to the game of cricket a most glorious bowling action that, fortunately for generations to come, has been captured over and over on film and videotape. If only we could sit back, without fear of loss, and savour now Tibby Cotter and Tom Richardson in action, hurling them down at MacLaren and Trumper at the turn of the century.

Jeff Thomson, built like a young Johnny Weissmuller, starts his run-up at the trot, without the thrust that the angular Bob Willis or the tiger-like Andy Roberts impart, so similar to a jet-plane wasting no time along the runway. By contrast Thommo's approach is casual at first, with only the flop of the light brown mane to catch the eye. There is a barely perceptible but crucial acceleration, at which point the enormous shoulders become more noticeable. Then comes the cocking of the catapult, the flinging back of the elastic right arm, with the sliding of the right foot behind rather than in front of the left. Now side-on as no orthodox bowler could be, he kicks out his left leg, the limb that brought so many wingers and inside-forwards to grief. Still the batsman has seen nothing worthwhile of the ball, though it shows for a micro-second, blood-red against his cream flannels, as he holds it by his rear before the final supercharged sweep of the arm. The mouth stretches grotesquely; the eyes protrude; the hair stands up like a cock's comb. He hurls himself almost off his feet, but the braced left leg absorbs the impact, giving way to the right as it wheels through, the body already well on the way to recovery, to balance.

Down at the other end a fresh set of problems for others has been created. That hard, round, leather lump will have travelled at over 145 kilometres per hour (90 mph) down the sickeningly short distance of 20 metres (22 yards) less the crease areas, more than likely bucking up savagely off a reasonable length, and veering off course, as if the batsman hadn't enough trouble. If the screaming ball passes the batsman, by design or otherwise, and misses the stumps, someone like Rodney Marsh has to intercept it. The wicketkeepers' grimaces over the years when taking Thommo have not all been for the benefit of the gallery.

That is Thommo the Tornado, Terror Thommo. He loves bowling, and he thrives on success. He is patriotic, but his patriotism takes the form of deep loyalty to his mates as much as to the flag — certainly not to authority — something that goes back to Gallipoli and even further into Australia's relatively brief history.

In a way he is a boy who never grew up. I mean this in that his outlook is refreshingly simple. He wants nothing to do with politics, accountancy, indoor life, lawyers, incapacity through injury. Yet, like all of us, he has had to take his share of many of those things. Always afterwards he wants to head for the open, racing after wild pigs, perhaps, to tone up the reflexes, or crashing into the cleansing waves of the Pacific.

It was my considered opinion that the only way to tell his story at all acceptably and without deception was for Jeff to say what he wanted to say, with prompting where it mattered, and for his collaborator to build around this. Quite apart from the problem of his memory — which is typically loose on his performances on the field and which leads him again and again to say 'You'd better check with Greg about that. He'd know' or 'Ask Dennis. He's bound to remember all about that' — there was the snag that he isn't the most lucid of raconteurs. Add to this the journalistic contortions of converting very rude words (when he gets excited about something, as with the bank robbery or his assault on the Sri Lanka batsmen) into something acceptable yet believable; add to this the decision-making involved in allowing not-so-very-rude words, hoping they would not offend fathers and uncles of young readers — or indeed the young readers themselves — and you have some idea of the difficulties faced at the planning stages.

The words attributed to him in this book are his, and there are tape recordings to prove it. Just as the numerous wickets he has taken for his State and his country are his, and the figures are there to prove it. He has been got at, unquestionably. He has himself to blame for certain mistakes, unquestionably. He has been the fastest bowler in the universe, unquestionably. As he finishes his last tape cassette he turns to the resumption of his career now that the division in Australian cricket has ended, and shows all the old determination to be tops again.

I was not with him when he added his comments on the World Series tour of West Indies and on the compromise between the Australian Cricket Board and WSC. He signed off like a man collecting his belongings at the prison exit: 'That's it, Frithy. That's all you're getting. There ain't no more. If you wanna ring me, don't, 'cos I won't be home. I'll be out fishing, mate. Lenny Pascoe and his wife, myself and Cheryl, we're leaving for Cairns for two months. So if you've got any messages I'd suggest you put 'em in a bottle, seal it and throw it in the sea. It might float up somehow to the Barrier Reef.'

No more messages, Jeff, old son. Except watch your waistline while you take things easy. A certain Yorkshireman reckoned he was The Finest Bloody Fast Bowler That Ever Drew Breath. Given another series or two like the unforgettable 1974-75 and the title might be yours.

CHAPTER 1
Silence in Court

The beach, the bush, the Brisbane Cricket Ground — but if there is one place Jeff Thomson would never feel at home it is the courtroom. Yet there he was, boxed in for twelve days in October 1978, while his immediate playing future was decided. Could he join World Series Cricket or was the Australian Cricket Board to hold him to its contract? When judgment was handed down, Thommo, with apparent nonchalance, was sitting at the back of the court, reading a fishing magazine.

What was this outdoor man, one half of the famous Lillee-Thomson express duo, doing in court in the first place? The story went back over a year, to the time when almost all the Australian Test team and several fringe players had signed to join media baron Kerry Packer's rebel enterprise. Denied exclusive television rights to Australian cricket, Packer and his advisers set about establishing their own series of matches. Several million dollars were invested, and by the end of 1977 there were over fifty players involved. Thomson's contract was worth $35,000 per annum for three years.

The complication was that he was already under contract to radio station 4IP in Queensland, and on July 28, 1977, just before the start of the Trent Bridge Test match against England, he announced he was tearing up his Packer contract. 'I didn't think it would interfere in any way with my cricket career, but it has, so I have withdrawn.'

There were later attempts by the Packer organisation to get him to change his mind, but the decision stuck . . . until he played for the depleted Australian Test team in a home series against India and on tour in West Indies. It was a different game from the one he had grown used to. No longer were the Chappell brothers there to spur him on, or Dennis Lillee, his alter ego, or Rod Marsh, to humour him and bully him and encourage him. Nor were Australia winning Test after Test.

Thommo became discouraged, retired, then attempted a comeback straight into the arms of Packer's World Series Cricket and of his old pals. The Australian Cricket Board were not going to stand for that, and were eventually successful in obtaining an order restraining Thomson from playing for World Series before March 31, 1979.

He was in the witness box for twelve hours in all, and suffered — not only because it was no natural habitat for him, but because the spotlight was put on inconsistencies in his claims. At times he was confused, and sometimes he misunderstood Counsel's questions. Hiccoughs occurred such as: Q. At about that time did you receive a telephone call from Mr McCarthy? A. October — I would have received it. Q. Or about this time? A. Not early in October. I was phoned up by Bill later in that month. Q. By Bill you mean Mr McCarthy? A. Yes.

It was an agonised chapter of details forgotten by him, of people and places unfixed chronologically, and contracts, schedules and declarations signed without having been read and with no copies left with the signatory. He was pushed to recall exact amounts paid to him by 4IP and the Board, though he would occasionally surprise with a specific sum, as when questioned on the amount he received from Benson & Hedges through the Board upon his return from the tour of West Indies. Was it approximately $2000-odd? He replied: '$2887 I think the figure was.'

When it came to examining his current financial state, he was asked if he was supporting Cheryl, his wife, a professional model: 'I'd say it would probably be the other way round,' he replied.

He told the court that judgments against him at that moment, in relation to the failed sports shop venture, totalled around $23,000. Besides that there was $24,000 owing to the tax man.

Part of his argument for quitting Test cricket was that the heavy schedule of matches ahead would leave him very little time with his wife. 'It's just not on. I think I'd be single in no time flat,' he said. 'Single, you mean matrimonially?' followed up Mr Hughes, QC. 'Yes. Which does not appeal to me at all.'

Then came the expression of his fear that he would be overworked as a fast bowler, lose his power and appeal, and, as a consequence, his market value. It was put as only he could put it:

'I am supposed to be the fastest bowler in the world. That is my go. That is where I obtain money. That is where I obtain a following and so on which gets me my contracts, you know, publicity, the works. I found that since I signed with the Board from November my ability to stay as a fast bowler was hindered due to the fact that I had to bowl all day, and nobody can bowl 100 miles an hour all day. So straight away my value was lost.'

He explained his desire to join World Series, 'back with the fellows I have always played with in those games and you bowl four or five overs off'.

Later on figures were produced which established that Thommo, under Bobby Simpson's captaincy in the Tests in West Indies, had bowled only 19.4 per cent of Australia's overs, which rather weakened his claim that he was being burnt out in the cause.

Things became uncomfortable for him again as Mr McHugh, QC, for the Board, asked him if, having entered into an agreement but not having read its contents at the time, he felt, as an honourable man, entitled to refuse to carry it out? When asked if he would sign a letter written on his behalf without reading it first, he replied, 'I have written very few letters on my behalf in my time.'

He must now have been yearning more than ever to canter down the beach and plunge headlong into the surf.

There were moments when he pinged in a cheeky bouncer of his own, as when he was asked in cross-examination if he had been playing soccer: **Q.** 'In a team?' **A.** 'A bit hard not to.'

And later: **Q.** 'Your style of bowling attracts a tremendous spectator interest, does it not?' **A.** 'Whatever turns them on, yes.'

Q. 'Frequently bowling at the batsman?' **A.** 'I don't bowl at the fieldsmen.'

Q. 'What about bowling at the batsman's body? Ever do that?' **A.** 'The ball slipped occasionally . . . I bowl where I think he finds it most difficult to play a shot. I don't have to bowl to the middle of his bat.'

He lost further ground over an admission that when Bob Parish, chairman of the Australian Cricket Board, had rung him on July 5, 1978 and asked him if he would be playing for Queensland and Australia in the coming season, he had answered, 'Yes, sure.' The fact was that he 'didn't quite believe I'd play for Australia because I wasn't happy'. He was also already immersed in negotiations with World Series Cricket. Mr McHugh then asked him if he thought there was anything reprehensible about making a false statement to the chairman of the ACB, to which he replied: 'At that time I had had a million people bothering me with phone calls and I was just glad to say yeah, yeah, yeah. . . . I am not quite sure of what I said on that day, to be absolutely correct, because I was just sick and tired of every Joe Blow ringing me up.'

Q. 'Mr Parish is not "every Joe Blow", is he?' **A.** 'No.'

One of the most significant of the exchanges was: 'Do you think you act a little irresponsibly occasionally?' To which Thommo replied, 'I probably trust too many people.'

Another characteristic phrase, heard more than once, was 'I just play cricket, and that's it.'

And another: **Q.** 'Would you agree with me that you have a very poor memory?' **A.** 'Where some things are concerned.'

He struggled to recall details of the Board contract prepared for the tour of West Indies early in 1978; when it was handed to him; what clauses it contained; how amendments were initialled, and so on. But he did remember Ken Mulcahy, station manager of 4IP, reminding him of his obligation to 4IP. 'Look,' he said Mulcahy told him, 'you have to tour.'

Elaborating, he recalled: 'He wanted me to go on that tour so that — to get a pat on the back when I was there, and I was going to be the vice-captain. It did not matter that I did not want to go, and my wife was away from home, and if I went it was worthless to me. . . . He virtually gave me the standover treatment.'

One of Thommo's major hot-spots was coming up now. It concerned his attitude to the Press. Counsel for the plaintiff asked him: 'Do you recall being spoken to by a journalist, Simunovich?'

'He rings up every blasted day just about,' said Thommo, 'him and all the rest.'

'You have a low opinion of journalists, have you?'

'Yes. They get on my goat most times.'

'You said to Simunovich it was a casual approach: "I was asked if I was interested in playing with WSC. I am sure that if I had said yes a firm offer would have been made." That is what you said to him when he spoke to you on the night of July 26, didn't you?'

'I can't remember if I said that. I would have told him anything to get rid of him.'

'Including a lie?'

'Including a lie. I didn't think I had to tell him anything.'

'No, but there is a difference between telling him nothing and telling him a lie, isn't there?' pressed Mr McHugh.

'Yes, I suppose there is.'

'And you preferred to tell him a lie?'

'He would have kept ringing me up until he got an answer and that was it. They never print what you tell them. Even if I told them the truth, or tell them the truth, they usually write lies anyway.'

He denied he kept quiet about the WSC agreement because he had a guilty conscience; he was, he said, just sticking to the agreement to keep it quiet.

When the matter of his big spending came up, the newspapers had a field day, and public sympathy went down a further few points. The $660 a month he had laid out on a Dino Ferrari motor car — a large chunk of his earnings after tax — became the talk of the nation. Then there were the phone bills. Much of the Benson & Hedges $2800 went towards them. Thommo reckoned he spent about $2300 on phone calls to his wife while he was on tour in West Indies.

Mr Justice Kearney eventually handed down his ruling on November 3, and Jeff Thomson was banned from playing for World Series Cricket during the 1978-79 Australian season. The upholding of the period to which he was committed to play for no unauthorised team also effectively prevented him from playing for WSC in West Indies, though the Board freed him from the contract shortly before the tour began, and he went with the WSC Australian team after all. The gesture was seen as a goodwill move on the part of the Board, and it also saved them some legal costs which an appeal by WSC and Thomson would inevitably have incurred.

So the Australian Cricket Board, with a compromise settlement with WSC still uncertain, perhaps unexpected, and — to our knowledge today — still over half a year away, had scored a useful victory. Mr Justice Kearney had found that while the November 1977 ACB contract was an unreasonable restraint of trade, and was therefore unenforceable, the further contract, prepared for the Australian tour of West Indies early in 1978, and duly signed by Thomson and all the other players in the side, was valid.

On the personal level, Thommo had been branded as 'arrogant, a liar, and irresponsible about money and other matters' by Mr McHugh, the Board's Counsel. To which Mr Conti, QC, representing Thomson, responded in his final submissions to the judge by saying: 'If the Board and Mr Parish are *bona fide* in the view that he is irresponsible and arrogant, then it rebounds against their credit to have Thomson in the team and as captain.'

That night, after the Equity Court decision against him in Sydney, Jeff Thomson drove to the Gold Coast to collect Cheryl. He was over the speed limit when a traffic cop intercepted him. He was fined $20, rounding off a memorable period in his life. If there was a consolation it was that Cheryl won the annual Concourse d'Elegance for fashion models with cars.

CHAPTER 2

Cloak and Dagger

Queensland solicitor Frank Gardiner has had a big hand in guiding Jeff Thomson's affairs. He went as 4IP's emissary in 1977 to England to explain the dangers of joining World Series Cricket (the company was then known as JP Sports Pty Ltd). Thommo, his 4IP contract threatened, duly pulled out of Packer cricket. About a year later Gardiner was trying to sort out Thommo's affairs once again, this time endeavouring to see him through a clean break with the Australian Cricket Board and into employment with World Series Cricket. He also set up for him the Thomson family trust, a company called Global Sportsman Pty Ltd.

Early in 1979 he explained Thommo's financial plight, beginning with the story of the two sports shops opened by Jeff, his brother Greg, and a man named Corbett:

They formed a company, and purchased various stock on credit around the place, and Jeff, as a director of the company, signed personal guarantees for rent and things like that; all the directors signed.

About that time Jeff was working hard to get his damaged shoulder back into shape to make the trip to England with the Australian Test team. Shortly after his marriage he had been in collision with one of his fieldsmen and put his shoulder out very badly. He received no compensation whatsoever from the Australian Cricket Board. He didn't participate in the Centenary Test. He got no monies whatsoever, apart from his medical bills paid. So he worked hard at getting fit to make that '77 tour, but as he was uncertain about his future he went into these stores. It wasn't his idea originally. The other two were to run them and Jeff was to lend his name to them, and attend the shops from time to time for promotional purposes.

He eventually made selection for that touring side, and when he joined the team at the airport a chap asked him if he was Jeff Thomson. He said he was, and was presented with a writ. The Brisbane stores both went into liquidation at that time. There was nothing he could do. He'd had nothing to do with the managing of the shops. He'd just put his money in and lent his name to it, but because he was Jeff Thomson, the personality, all the creditors imagined him to be the man of substance, and so they all sued him personally under the guarantee. He was stuck with it. Everyone had lobbed their actions against him. Soon he had one judgment against him for about $14,000 in rent and a series of others taking the full total through to about $30,000 from that trading venture.

Besides this, he had been persuaded by his employers, 4IP, to have a top-class car to help build up the image of Thomson the personality. It was part of the business of presenting a loud, colourful image, which would reflect back onto the radio station and its involvement in Queensland cricket. That was all part of the concept.

While Jeff was touring England in 1977 we found out he had signed for Kerry Packer, *and I went across there and spoke to him, and he made a decision to rejoin 4IP at a lesser contract. We met at Leicester and Nottingham, and I made the point that we didn't care which way he went. We wanted him to think carefully about what he intended to do, but no matter what, his contract with 4IP was at that time considered by us to be repudiated by him, and we were accepting such repudiation. The ten-year contract was gone and finished. I also told him that if he so desired, we would enter into a new contract with him which was safe and which was certain. I pointed out that with World Series Cricket he had no guarantees at that time, and that it was only a $98 company. He couldn't say for certain whether he would be looked after.*

On that basis, he came back to me an hour later and said on what I considered as acceptable terms, and he signed it. Then we wrote to the Packer organisation and told them that we were out of it. Money paid to Jeff was repaid to World Series.

The earlier 4IP contract was something of an illusion as far as its value went. They said, in effect, we're giving you a car, and that's worth so much a week to you, and if you receive so much a week clear in your hand that would be the equivalent of so much extra, taxable. Say they put $5000 on the use of the car: they'd say, that's $5000 after tax, so therefore before tax that would be about $9000 or $10,000. Everything he ever got was computed in that way.

It's not true that Jeff ever had lots of money. When he was on about 400 or 500 bucks a week he had a good time, and as he says himself, 'I don't regret one bit of it. I had a good time. It was most enjoyable.' It's only after you get married that you realise that some of that money would have come in useful.

As for tax liability, he had a couple of good years with 4IP and from cricket earnings, but his tax year 1977-78 was what you might call a 'killer-diller'. There was just no provision for any tax there. Big income, no tax paid, so his provisional tax together with the tax that he actually has to pay for the subsequent year became enormous — about $22,000. He is in no position to pay that.

Before picking up Jeff Thomson's life story from its cradle and taking it through its rumbustious days of youth into the glory years of his successes for Australia, there is one further stretch of murky water to cross, and Frank Gardiner, speaking early in 1979, now tells the story as he saw it — the story of alleged cloak-and-dagger goings-on in the usually serene, sunlit and stable environs of Brisbane:

Just before the Australian Cricket Board took legal action against Jeff Thomson, an approach by a large commercial radio station in Brisbane was made to Jeff, through me as well, by one of their representatives who knew very much what was happening, and said he had an 'in' with the Board, and this is what could be done. He was 99.99 per cent sure it would be done. Thommo as current vice-captain would be made captain if he stayed; secondly, they would guarantee that just before the first Test against the Englishmen, Rixon would be dropped and John Maclean would be put in, perhaps with two others from Queensland. Preference would be given to Maclean because Thommo got on so well with him; thirdly, they said not to worry about Simpson's presence in the matter. He was going to be dropped as well.

We told Mike Sheahan, the cricket-writer with the Melbourne Age, not to publish John Maclean's name as it might jeopardise his chances of being selected. We told him the story, but stressed the need not to mention names. Anyway, a few weeks later, when the team was announced, Maclean was in, Rixon out, the whole thing as forecast. I spoke to Mike Sheahan later, and said, 'That backs up what Jeff and I told you. That verifies what approaches were made to us, doesn't it?'

I believe that the Board told the Queensland Cricket Association to keep Thomson out in the cold. Therefore they had to give Queensland something. That's why Maclean, Carlson, Dymock and Cosier all came in. I think every one of them justified his selection, but it was a terrific upsurge for Queensland.

One thing that is absolutely unchallengeable is that Jeff Thomson, at all times, including during the court hearing, said that he was prepared and willing to play for Queensland. I called in to see the QCA secretary, Bill McCarthy, who knew I was coming to see him. I sat down and said, 'Right, now let's work out the situation for Thommo to play for Queensland.'

Bill said, 'Frank, I can't do anything other than arrange a conference between you, members of the Association, and our lawyer.' I said, 'Why not, for Christ's sake? All I want is for the QCA to say that they respect Thomson as a cricketer and a man, and they want him to continue to play for the State.'

He said, 'Frank, I can't talk to you. I can't even listen to what you're saying. I can't even put it to anybody.'

'This is bloody ridiculous,' I said. 'Listen, I'm going upstairs to have a drink in the Cricketers' Club. I'm tired. I've been in Sydney for four weeks on this court case. I'm going home to the Gold Coast and I'm going to swim all weekend, and I'm not coming back up here for anyone. Now if you want a bloody meeting or talk with me about Thomson playing, you'd better do it today.'

About half an hour later I got a phone call from Norm McMahon, the QCA chairman, telling me they wanted to talk, they wanted Thomson to play, etcetera, etcetera, but they were concerned about his situation with the Board. As far as they were concerned he was playing for Queensland, and that was it.

I told him that if they wanted to have a meeting, it had better be quick. But Norm McMahon said he was taking his wife out for their wedding anniversary. Could we meet in town at a solicitor's office? 'For you, Norm, I will,' I said. 'As a personal favour, since we've co-operated together over in England fairly well.'

We sat down in that office, with several people present, and I told him we wanted a letter to restore some of Jeff's self-respect, after the way the Board had attempted to destroy him as a person.

They couldn't give me an answer straightaway, so I said I would go back to the Cricketers' Club, have a beer over there, and then go back to the Gold Coast. Just as I was leaving, Bill McCarthy came in and said, 'Look, I've got something here for you.'

They'd toned down the letter that I'd originally suggested, but it still covered the points I wanted covered — that they and the team were happy to have Jeff Thomson playing for Queensland. That letter was released almost immediately and published in most of the newspapers.

But would you believe what followed! There was a story in the Brisbane Courier Mail *claiming that Thomson had demanded $50,000 from the QCA to play for Queensland! An 'informed source' story of this alleged demand followed. Jeff and I denied it emphatically, but the story stayed in circulation. It was totally untrue. That meeting had concerned the letter alone; there was no mention of money at all. It really hurt both of us, and it showed up the standard of journalism where they don't even bother to ring up the other side and publish the denial.*

A week or two later, Norm McMahon denied that any such demand had been made. But they didn't do it that day, *which made me very unhappy with the QCA. I should have thought they had enough integrity to deny that story immediately.*

When Jeff played for Queensland against South Australia in the first Gillette Cup match of the season, he got a bit of a roasting from the crowd for demanding fifty million, and all the rest of it, and that worked him up good and proper. He killed 'em. He took 6 for 18.

After that, we went down to Sydney for the Appeal case. I had let it be known, through journalist David Falkenmire, that Jeff would be available for all Queensland's matches, except where there was a clash with promotional activities for the company by which he was employed — Global Sportsman Pty Ltd, a family trust company which I had set up for him. But it now became clear that Jeff would not be available for that opening Shield game because we had reason to believe that the court's decision would be handed down around the time that the match would commence. His company required him to be there in Sydney whichever way it went. One of the newspapers came back with some story about his presence not being legally necessary in court. This was not rele-

vant. His employer wanted him there for the purpose of being seen to accept the decision, be it favourable or otherwise. He wasn't going away to hide in a corner.

With that in mind, we informed the QCA that Thomson would probably not be available. Soon we were able to say that he definitely would not be available, because judgment was imminent, so we'd been informed.

They refused to accept our statement, and one paper was saying he would be available, another that he wouldn't.

We went to Sydney and took the decision. As soon as we got back to Brisbane, Jeff reiterated that he was prepared to play for Queensland. Initially he said he was going fishing. But then he came back and said, 'Look, I've always said I'll play for Queensland. I'll stick to it.'

I told the Press that he was available, and that World Series Cricket had agreed to Jeff's playing for the State for the rest of the season, pending the outcome of the appeal, and providing it didn't clash with any promotional duties he had — not cricket duties — promotional duties. This was reported all over the place, but the QCA took no notice of that. They kept saying that Thomson hadn't made himself available.

Finally, I told Jeff that nobody was taking any notice. So he rang the QCA and told them that he was available. Fine. So Bill McCarthy, the secretary, wrote a letter to the chairman of selectors just before the match against the Englishmen, saying that Thomson was available. Jeff had made it clear that he couldn't attend a pre-match practice because he was competing in the Fastest Bowler in the World contest in Perth. But he would be available for practice straight afterwards. We were told that all this was made clear in the secretary's letter to Ern Toovey, the chairman of selectors.

The selectors met and chose their team, and Jeff Thomson was omitted. No reasons were given. I rang Bill McCarthy shortly afterwards and asked why Jeff wasn't selected, and he said, 'I've got no idea, Frank.'

'If he turns up for practice this afternoon,' I said, 'as he might well do, because he mightn't know about the decision, I don't want him to be embarrassed, to look a goose, having been dropped from the side.'

Jeff Thomson has not been selected to play for Queensland since, and no reason has ever been given.

I understand it was a three-two vote by the selectors. Since then there has been one further overture by the QCA to get Jeff to play again, but before a meeting could be arranged between us, two members of the Association who were trying to do the right thing were apparently overborne by the more conservative elements who had adopted the attitude of 'If he's going to play for World Series Cricket, why should we pick him now? We don't want him and we're not going to let anyone else have him.'

CHAPTER 3

Reluctant Young Champ

Thommo's memories of his boyhood and teenage years are probably sharper than those of the places he has visited and the people he has met while playing cricket for New South Wales, Queensland and Australia.

We talked and taped in the cavernous dressing-room at VFL Park, Melbourne during a WSC Supertest, where Jeff was making a 'personal appearance', and in the claustrophobic physio room, where the battered but indestructible shoulder had its massage. We pursued things further at his parents' place at Bankstown, an outer western suburb of Sydney, where his father watched with pride as Jeff's nephew bowled on the wide, flat expanse of coarse lawn at the rear of the house, while inside other members of the family sweltered. The fan whirred and rotated its head as if unable to stand the heat much longer, and Cheryl reclined in an armchair utterly motionless — a still-life model now. The World Series match on television ensured a constant background hubbub, with the commentators getting excited and the lounge-room audience responding.

The occasional phut of a beer being opened kept us awake, but Thommo's eyes kept fixing upon the massive vivid yellow truck and boat in the front yard. He wanted to be off.

Mum had produced the scrapbooks which she had lovingly compiled over the years, and that was helpful.

'Righto, then,' said Thommo, 'let's get stuck in.' His story unfolded, and he became quite animated at times, especially when talking about his cars. And when the bank hold-up was being re-enacted I lost him for a time. He leapt from his seat to demonstrate, moved along the wall like Humphrey Bogart, and his voice receded almost out of range of the microphone. When he is anxious to please, he is like a nine-year-old choirboy: on this occasion as soon as he saw he'd fouled up the recording he came racing back to his seat, repentant, if only for five seconds.

Yes, he really enjoys a laugh when he gets into it. When the publisher had a preview of one of the tapes he said, half-jokingly, that we ought to issue a long-playing record instead of a book.

Reaching back a couple of decades, Thommo now takes up the tale:

It all began in the back yard. I came from a family of five boys —
Donny, Raymond, Gregory, myself, and Kevin — and my father, Don,
played cricket for many years. In fact he had the same type of bowling
action as mine. I remember that now when I think back to the cricket
we used to play in the back yard when I was a kid.

Dad was a very good cricketer. He played in the Bankstown district,
A grade juniors, but he had a bit of a hard time when he was young.
Money was short and he and Mum were young when they married. So
he didn't really want to play representative cricket. He always wanted
to play with his mates. Some of them, of course, went on to play
big-time cricket. Jack Fitzpatrick was one of them.

Dad came from Newtown and Mum, whose name is Doreen, came
from Redfern, both inner suburbs of Sydney. Mum used to take me to
watch the Old Man play cricket from as early as I can remember —
every Saturday afternoon, all over Bankstown and the surrounding
districts. At Condell Park Primary School I began playing myself, and
that's where I first met Lenny Pascoe. His name was Durtanovich then.
He used to go to another school in the area, and he was pretty fast. I
can't remember how the match went. It was only on a bush ground. I
reckoned I was quick then, and I've always been a fighter, so we tried to
get the better of each other.

At the age of nine or ten I was solidly built, but I hadn't shot up yet
like some other kids. Still, I was good enough to make my first
appearance in the 'big time' when I played on Saturday mornings for a
team called Padstow Pirates. The big noise around that time was a kid
called Billy Palmer, a really promising junior, perhaps the best in New
South Wales. They used to give him the wraps — Billy Palmer this,
Billy Palmer that. I was put on to bowl at the other end. I still had a lot
to learn, naturally. I'd only bowled in the back yard to that stage. But I
remember thinking: I'm gonna knock this bloke off! If they think he's
the best, *I'll show them!* He was about twelve, and used to play C grade
in the afternoon with the men. I can't remember who got the best
figures that day, but it shows you how competitive I was even when I
was wet behind the ears.

Anyway, Dad got me up to the North Bankstown club. I would've
started there but they didn't have any juniors until the early 1960s.
Season after season I won the bowling — most wickets, best average,
whipping a two-piece ball down on coir matting pitches (over concrete).
Dad's A grade mates helped, taking turns to umpire and saying, 'Look,
Jeff, just bowl to this bloke this way, or that way', and I could always
bowl where they wanted me to. I got millions of wickets.

But this was only second division, and there were always first division
clubs that wanted to snip me. But I couldn't be bothered moving,
because I was with me mates, fellas I knew, and Dad and his mates
were running the thing.

When I think about it, things haven't changed much. Being with me mates has always mattered a lot, and that's one of the main reasons why I wanted to leave Test cricket in 1978 and join World Series. You've got to enjoy what you're doing.

Getting back to those early days, I used to play *three games* on Saturday. I used to play Under-14s (even when I was only twelve) from about eight o'clock till about ten-thirty, and then I'd go and play for the Under-16s from eleven till one-thirty, then I'd go straight from that ground to the C grade men's match and play from two till six. Sometimes I'd have to run a mile to a mile-and-a-half from one ground to the next if Dad couldn't pick me up. Some days, with the luck of the toss, I'd be bowling in every game. It'd be nothing to bowl fifty-odd overs on a Saturday, and I never even felt it.

I also won a few trophies for batting — best aggregate. They're still at home. Not that I ever made a hundred. My highest score to this day in any form of cricket is 89 not out in first grade at school. We played the other school that was in contention for the competition, so it was a valuable knock. I've never ever worried about making a century. I just like to make enough runs to help the side along, and to make them quickly.

I wouldn't pretend to be an academic, but I finished in the top five at primary school and won the opportunity to choose from three secondary schools. My brother Greg had previously won a scholarship to Punchbowl High School, so I decided to go there too.

I broke away from all my mates now, and at Punchbowl I knew nobody. That's when I ran into Len Pascoe again. He lived nearby and automatically went to that school. We both turned up at the nets there to try out for the school sixth grade, and he got in but the teacher in charge — a music teacher; that's why I've never liked music teachers — didn't pick me. It really burnt me off. It was ridiculous. This guy just didn't like me. You know, music lessons and reading out notes and all that. I just didn't go for it, and because of that he didn't pick me. It was so stupid. I had to go down and play what they called 'house' cricket with all the other mugs who couldn't even hold a bat. I used to go down there and slog hundreds (I don't count them) and take ten wickets for nothing. It was ridiculous. I wasted a whole year that way.

Let me just point out here that I love music. It's just music teachers that I'm not too keen about. It depends on the occasion, but I love several kinds of music, and I've got a quad set and loads of LPs. I love ELO, Chicago, the Rolling Stones, Elton John, and especially the negro stuff. I like heavy rock, and when I was younger, in my surfing days, I used to go for Black Sabbath and Led Zeppelin. And like my co-author, I'm mad on the Beach Boys.

Back to school. In the second year at high school they had a different selector, and I played in the fifth grade. Now it all started to happen. I got heaps of wickets. The coach was Joe McCann, an ex-mayor of

Bankstown who'd become a schoolteacher. He was a good, friendly guy who maybe didn't know so much about the game.

It didn't take me long to get into the first-grade side, and I was in it for about three seasons, captaining it for the last couple, when we were undefeated. The school magazine shows that I took 9 for 3 against Belmore, and Len Pascoe took 8 for 21 against Birrong, following it with 7 for 45 against East Hills. My 9 for 3 included my first hat-trick, the first of a total of ten hat-tricks so far, I reckon, including one in Canada on the way over to England in 1975.

By 1967 I was also in the school first team at soccer, playing left-half. I was pretty strongly-built, and about this time I tried out for Melita Eagles, Newtown. I got into second grade, and was on the verge of getting into the first team. But I gave it away. It meant three nights a week training, and I had to drive all the way into town, Camperdown Oval. It got a bit of a drag, especially at a stage of my life when anything out of the ordinary I couldn't be bothered with. Playing cricket came naturally. I didn't have to train, didn't have to be super-fit, and I didn't have to spend three nights a week driving into town. So it was goodbye to serious football. I'd made a few quid and won a trophy, but from now on it was semi-social soccer for me.

It was in this friendly competition, called the Protestant Churches League (I think I played for some Church of England side), playing alongside my brother, that I got into a bit of strife. I was about twenty at the time. The refereeing was atrocious. Diabolical. I remember something had happened to upset me during the week, and I was really shirty that day. This ref just capped it off. I thought he was straightout cheating. Throughout my life I've always hated anyone who lies to me or tries to cheat me. I've got a very short temper, and that's the only thing that really burns me up. He just went a little bit too far this day. I just snapped. I laid one on him. The life ban has just recently been lifted.

I came back to soccer in 1978, playing for the Trident club in Brisbane and helping them to get up into the first division. I still take an interest in the game — not necessarily within Australia, but I follow the fortunes of English club Manchester United, as do thousands throughout the world.

Getting back to my cricket career, when I was playing for North Bankstown in the second division, a bloke came round one evening to try to get me to join Bankstown RSL club, that Len Pascoe played for. He said to my old man, 'Look, Don, he's not going to get anywhere playing second division. He gets heaps of wickets every week but nobody's ever worried about it. He should be playing better competition.'

I remember the old man telling him not to worry about it, and to leave the kid alone. He was a bit surprised when I said 'I want to play.' He said, 'If you want to play, that's okay.' So I did. I played for

Bankstown RSL with Lenny, and that's how it all started.

About ten years later we were opening the bowling together for Australia in the Jubilee Test match at Lord's!

The Bankstown RSL Under-16 side, with Lenny and me as their fast bowlers, just about ruled the roost. There was only one other real side in it, and that was Bankstown Sports. When we played each other there were some great old tussles. It was on for young and old. At the same time I got picked for the A.W. Green Shield team (Under-16s) for Bankstown, coached by Dickie McDermot, who played first-grade Rugby League for Canterbury-Bankstown and Bankstown grade cricket. This was when I joined forces again with Billy Palmer. We opened the bowling, and Len Pascoe was sometimes twelfth man — that's how good a side we had.

We won the Green Shield that season, 1965-66, after beating Western Suburbs in a play-off at Drummoyne Oval. Billy Palmer made most runs and took most wickets in the competition, but my bowling average (10.53 for 17 wickets) was lower. The New South Wales Cricket Year Book shows a young bloke called Kerry O'Keeffe at the top of the bowling. He took 33 wickets at less than ten apiece with his leg-spinners for St George. My name is spelt with a 'p' in it. That's something I've had to put up with nearly all my life.

The next step, in the following season, was to play for Bankstown C grade in the Municipal and Shire competition. Lenny and I were told to go to the net trials at the start of the season, and we found ourselves practising with fellas like Ian King, the aboriginal fast bowler, Grahame Thomas, who played for Australia as a batsman, and Ronnie Briggs, who played for the State.

Anyway, Lenny and I opened the bowling for this C-grade side, and we won the competition, beating Sydney in the final game. Lenny took nearly 60 wickets at less than seven each, and I got 47 at 8½. I remember in one match, out at Mascot, I took 5 for 6, and me mate got hit around — he took 5 for 12!

I was still at school — captain of the first team. It was great fun. I didn't do so much bowling then. I was a lazy captain. I just let Lenny do it all.

I used to do heaps of things when I was in my teens, including fishing. Ever since the day I was born, I think, I always wanted a boat. I was always dreaming of boats, wanted them as toys when I was a kid. When I was about fourteen I joined the New South Wales Amateur Fishing Association, with my brother Greg. We were so keen we'd go to the meetings in the city, and after Greg had finished work and I'd got out of school we'd go off fishing, and sometimes fish all through the night. We'd start late in the afternoon and go through to three in the morning.

We used to go out and stand on the ocean rocks, hanging on to a metal spike while the surf rolled all over us. We went to some really dangerous spots. Cape Banks is so treacherous that thirty-eight blokes have been washed away there. If you get taken there, you can say goodbye, unless you're a bloody Channel swimmer or something. You'd have to swim right the way round the bay, and the current's usually against you.

If you asked me to fish all night now, I wouldn't do it. But I'd go out in the boat, anywhere you like. Less risky. I remember once, at Narrabeen, we went out on this ledge, with a channel running alongside of it, a couple of feet wide. Most of the channel was shallow, one part of it was a hole! We'd caught a few fish, then as this wave came at me I turned around and ran, just mucking around, and I took the short-cut too quick and fell in the deep part. There I was, suddenly looking eye to eye with this bloody great wave coming at me. You've never seen a bloke move so fast. I was up and out like a rocket, and my brother was laughing his head off. We had a few hairy moments in those years, but that was the worst one. Australia might almost have needed someone else to take the new ball with Dennis Lillee in the 1970s!

It was ridiculous the number of things I used to do in a day — four games of soccer a week, fishing, surfing. My brother was a lifesaver, and at weekends, when I was about twelve, we used to go down to the south coast, near Thirroul, and surf a lot. I used a board in those days, but later on I preferred body-surfing.

School became a drag to me when I was about sixteen. I'd passed my School Certificate, and went on for the extra two years for the High School Certificate. It was the worst thing I ever did. The only reason I went on was for sport. I had just one exercise book for all my lessons. I didn't write in it. I didn't do any homework either, and I didn't care what else was going on in the world.

I was school athletics champion, cricket captain, picked in the zone side for soccer and for the CHS rep team, which I never turned up to because soccer just didn't have that extra bit of attraction that cricket had for me. The game just didn't have the flair in Australia in those days. One year, when injury kept me out of cricket, I played first-grade hockey — and got picked in the zone team. First time I'd ever played hockey, but I found it so easy.

My eldest brother used to do a lot of rally-driving, and we used to go along with him. Then I decided to give it a go. We won a few things, taking part with the Liverpool Car Club out at the old Warwick Farm raceway. I was only young, and I used to scream round like buggery. I'd only had the Mini Cooper-S a few weeks when I smashed it up and virtually wrote it off. I never hit anyone. I just went off the road, over a gutter and off into the bushes, mowing down a few trees just out the back of Bankstown. All the wheels were torn off except one, and I sat there and looked at my poor car and thought, Geez, I'm paying the thing off still, so what am I going to do here?

I couldn't afford to get anyone to fix it, so I got it back home and pulled it apart completely, everything that moved, and rebuilt it. I got the panels straightened and rubbed it back. Kevin, my younger brother, is a top mechanic. He's come first in every exam he's ever done on the subject, and Donny was the boss of a big car dealership and service place when he was only twenty-one.

British Leyland were racing a few Minis out here then, and I built it to their specifications, put it all together myself, and used it for a while. Then I sold it to a bloke locally and he used it for rallying. I couldn't afford rallying really when I was in my late teens.

It's funny, but I never followed the big cricket matches when I was younger. I never went to a Test match or a Shield match. The first ones I saw were the first ones I played in. I watched a bit on television, and remember the tied Test against West Indies in '60-61. My hero at that time would probably have been Freddie Trueman. Not that I've ever idolised any cricketer. I don't think of anyone as being better than me. My goal has always been to be the best, so that the others can worry about being as good as me. It's not meant to be a big-headed attitude, just the best you can have as a sportsman, if you want to be Number One. No good thinking that someone else is better than you. That way you're defeated before you start. I'll never admit that until the day I start losing it. And then I still won't admit it. I'll just give it away, and play friendly cricket. If there is such a thing.

The next couple of seasons saw us move up in the grades at Bankstown. While Lenny played fourths, I was in the thirds, with the occasional game in the seconds. Eventually it was out of me or Billy Palmer who made it into the firsts. He was an all-rounder, which meant I had to bowl bloody well to knock him out of the side. I'd grown by now. I was a pretty big fellow. And at the pre-season nets, for grade selection, I don't know how many times I bowled him out. Shot him to pieces. That was the end. I was a first-grade bowler.

The next bit of excitement came when I was chosen in the New South Wales squad. I was still only seventeen, but the selectors must have seen something there. I didn't actually make the State team just yet, of course, but I remember practising with players like Brian Taber, Dave Renneberg, Gordon Goffet, Alan Turner.

At eighteen I was sixth in the overall grade averages, but Lenny was to beat me into the New South Wales Colts side. He played against Queensland in 1969-70, but things went bad for me between when I was seventeen and twenty-one.

What happened during that time? Well, Lenny and myself were at the stage where girls came into it. I started to chase girls. I hadn't up to that stage. It used to be a case of sport, totally and utterly. Give me a game of anything and I'd give you a game to the death, you know, no matter what it was. Then we started to wander. We used to love surfing — Maroubra Beach, The Entrance, Nora Heads, Soldiers Beach, Garie Beach. We'd go away for weekends, doing the usual teenage bit where you go to parties, booze on and get drunk. It didn't affect our cricket. We still bowled a hundred per cent. But we used to roll up late occasionally, and we got into trouble.

After my first year in first grade, when I did really well, I began to think Ah, this is easy. This is a warning I'd give to any young player whose head gets a bit big.

Lenny and I were lucky with our captain at Bankstown when we started in the firsts. He was Bob Madden, a great all-round sportsman who played cricket for New South Wales and soccer for Australia. But he was nearing the end of his career. At the same time, it began to look as if mine wasn't exactly taking off. I'll admit I'd started to bludge. I'd pick up a couple of wickets, but I just didn't have it with me. When things didn't go right I sort of slumped. I'd think, Geez, what's going wrong? I can't be bothered worrying about it. I'd rather go surfing. Suddenly I found myself dropped into third grade.

One fateful afternoon, when we were due to play St George, on a really hot day, I said to my brother Greg, 'I'm not going. Let's go fishing. Or let's go to the beach.'

He said, 'No, mate. You'd better get to the cricket.'

So I said, 'Stuff cricket. I've been dropped to third grade. I can't be bothered.'

In the previous match, I think it was against Petersham, the captain — I didn't care for him all that much — he ran me out for no score and I hardly got a bowl. So I was pretty fed up with it all. But now Mum stepped in and said to Greg, 'You take him out to the cricket.' So he took me over in his red EH Holden car.

We got there late, but the field was deserted. I thought, Hello, what's going on here? But it turned out that one of the umpires had been delayed. Everything was clicking in my favour. There was I, ready for someone to chip me about being late. And then I definitely would've walked out.

The captain simply said, 'We're bowling, Thommo. Get your gear on quick.' I did just that, had four separate bowling spells that afternoon, and while no-one else even looked like getting a wicket, I finished with all ten for 35. I think I got eight clean-bowled and two lbw. There might have been a hat-trick in that lot too.

Can't remember what I did in the second dig — 5 for 10 or something. Bit of a bloody anticlimax anyway!

It was good to knock off St George with an outright victory. They usually won most of the lower grade competitions. Anyway, from there I soon moved up back to first grade, and Lenny and I took wickets and got asked to play in Metropolitan representative matches and all that sort of thing. We always got asked to practise with the State squad too. But we went only about once every two weeks, and they held that against us. That was crap, because if you're good enough you should be picked.

We tried like Hell. Every season we absolutely killed 'em. We got results. Batsmen were scared to play us. Geez, some of the injuries!

One of the worst was the son of the late Reg Ledwidge, the Test umpire. I'd really snapped and I was out to show people what I was made of. It wasn't actually a bouncer, but it was bloody fast and it smashed him straight in the eye. It was frightening to see this bloke just screaming and shaking, and the pitch was splattered with blood as it poured through his fingers. He was in the intensive-care unit of the hospital for a week. Like so many blokes, he just hadn't had time to move out of the way of the ball, even though the pitch at Bankstown was pretty dead.

I never let this sort of thing put me off, because, all right, this is my aggression. The batsman's got a bat and he can hit the ball and do what he likes to me. I don't mean to hit him, even though I could if I wanted to — especially now, when I'm bowling faster and more accurately than ever in my life.

The event that changed my thinking on this was the death of my flat-mate, Martin Bedkober. I've had a different attitude towards fast bowling since then. Martin was killed in December 1975 when he was hit in the chest by a fastish bowler in a club match in Brisbane. He collapsed at the wicket and died two hours later in Royal Brisbane Hospital.

I was playing for Australia against West Indies at the time, in Perth, and I got back to Sydney in time for his funeral. He had gone north at the same time as Ian Davis and myself, in an attempt to make the Queensland State side. It was an awful tragedy.

As I say, there's no point trying to knock a bloke out. It's more of a thrill to me to see the stumps go over. I'd rather bowl 'em out than knock 'em out.

Getting back to my problems when I was on the verge of something big — we'd turn up for a game straight from the beach, we'd have salt in our hair, we'd have our cricket boots under our arms, our creams under the other, no bags, no nothing, shorts on, no shirt, pair of thongs. That's how we'd turn up for State squad practice. It's always been my motto that it doesn't matter what you look like or what you're dressed like, it's results that count — delivering the goods.

The captains didn't like it. Why don't you do this, they'd say, and why don't you do that. But I just told 'em to piss off.

I suppose since then I've bent those rules a little bit. But not much. It might have set me back a few years, but I still did my own thing. I'm a kind of rebel, I suppose, but it all depends on what you classify as a 'rebel'.

So, I had five years of getting wickets and breaking bones and upsetting captains and scaring Christ out of everyone that ever walked onto our particular cricket field in Sydney — but not making the New South Wales side. I don't regret it. I do what I feel like doing as I feel like doing it — and always have done. When the time came for me to straighten out, when I was made vice-captain of Australia during the 1977-78 season, I changed appreciably then. I don't think anyone could put a black mark against me, and I think I performed the vice-captaincy duties pretty well — I don't really know. You'd have to ask

Fred Bennett, the manager, or Bob Simpson, the captain. It was a great honour, and I gave it my all.

I got the nod from the selectors at last at the start of the 1972-73 season after I'd topped the bowling averages for the whole of the Sydney grade competition the previous season, with 52 wickets at 13.90. They picked me to play against Queensland at Brisbane.

We lobbed up there for the game, but it had poured rain for days, and the Gabba ground was very wet. I was never so keen to really do well, but I didn't know what to expect either. For instance, I was up against Sam Trimble, a batsman I'd always looked up to. But I didn't know his likes and dislikes.

I made a lot of stupid, raw statements to the newspapers along those lines — you know, what's a fella expected to do against a batsman whose weaknesses I didn't know, and all that crap. Anyway, I was rooming with John Benaud, our captain, and though I used to love having a drink even then, I wouldn't have one. I just didn't want to put a foot wrong — wouldn't have swallowed a beer if you gave me a hundred dollars.

I sat in that bloody motel room for two days, until John said, 'Look, Thommo, this is not going to do you any good. It's raining like buggery. Get out and get pissed tonight. It'll do you the world of good. You're a bundle of nerves.'

So I went to a disco with Alan Turner, Ron Crippin and Steve Bernard, and we raged all night and got pretty drunk because it was a long session. I forget when it closed, but it seemed like a long time, because I hadn't had a drink for a while. Anyway, we found our way across the Storey Bridge and up Main Street to the motel, three-quarters of a mile but it seemed a bloody long way when you're a bit unsteady at that time of night.

I remember waking up early with a hangover and feeling a bit dry. Got up and had a look out the window, and the sky was absolutely clear — usual Brisbane caper: flooded one day and red-hot the next. It was *bloody* hot. I remember that, 'Fitterun' Turner and I were out at six or seven in the morning in the swimming pool, trying to get a bit fresh.

We went down to the ground, and it was very hot and muggy. I remember the captains talking about when to start, and Clem Jones, who was the curator then, was telling them he didn't want to start just yet. He was still putting bags around the pitch and running rollers everywhere, but he chipped in to say that there was nothing wrong with the wicket, and they should get in and play. John Benaud told him that when he wanted his advice he'd ask for it, and he could quit sticking his bib in.

We batted and made nine for 174 (Geoff Dymock took five wickets), and when it was time to bowl, 'Benords' looked after me. After all, it was his fault. He'd told me to go out that night! I got Don Allen caught behind and had Alan Jones caught by Douggie Walters, and I think I had 2 for 8 off four overs when Benaud gave me a rest. I finished with 2 for 24 off eight, and the match was drawn.

Before the next Shield match I played for New South Wales Colts against Queensland at Sydney and bagged 5 for 79, Steve Rixon taking a couple of catches behind the stumps, then the Shield side went to Perth to play Western Australia. This marked my first confrontation with a fella who was going to have a lot to do with me during my career · — Dennis Lillee. The previous year he had knocked hell out of the Rest of the World side touring Australia, and then during the Australian tour of England he had done really well.

After football practice me and my mates used to go home to my place and play cards all night, listening to the Tests on the radio and having a drink. Me mates used to stir me up about Dennis bowling quick and all that, and the blokes on the radio were saying how quick he was bowling — he was the fastest thing out, etcetera. I think me mates thought I was real quick anyway, but they carried on stirring me up.

So I remembered all this when I came up against Lillee and Massie. This was my chance to show who's who and what's what. I used to really sling 'em then. I used to spray 'em around everywhere. Anyhow, we batted, and didn't do too well, and I came onto the WACA ground that evening and opened the bowling in front of that crowd, who are very 'aggro', very one-eyed. I came running in with the Fremantle Doctor blowing behind me, and Graeme Watson was opening the batting. He'd had that terrible blow in the face from a Tony Greig full-toss a year before. Anyway, I let him have it. One bouncer (I used to bowl big inswingers and leg-cutters in those days), it took off and came down miles down the leg side, and Ron Crippin ran backwards and caught it at deep leg slip. Didn't the crowd give me a serve over that! I was as nervous as buggery.

But that night I sat down and thought, Why should I be nervous? Geez, I'll show these blokes. Ever since, when something like that happens I just talk to myself and say, What have I got to be nervous about? I've got nothing to lose. Next day I got four wickets and 'Gus' Gilmour got five. Not bad against the WACAs, who were real strong.

I remember Dennis Lillee coming in. Doug Walters was fielding at cover, next to me, with the rest of the blokes all behind the wicket, catching. Dennis comes strutting in, real mean bugger, you know, the King, sort of thing. I thought, I'll show you.

I wasn't going to bounce him. Doug made sure of that. 'Don't bounce him, for Christ's sake,' he said. 'Don't worry about him,' I said. 'I'll soon fix him up!'

Anyway, Dennis got a four off me. I think it was an edge. So I really let one go. It got up off a length and smashed him on the gloves. He let go of his bat and held his hand and ran a single, and when he got up my end he said, 'I hope you can hold a f------ blade, pal!' I was grinning, and I said, 'Listen, pal, you've got the bat at the moment. Just get up the other end and see how f------ good you are!' And Doug had turned white as a ghost. He must have been pooping himself!

Those were the only words Dennis and I have ever had against one another. I got him caught by Brian Taber. Later on, when it was my turn to bat, Dennis bowled a couple of short ones that whistled past my chin, but I got 16 — all fours, slogging — before he bowled me with a slower one.

I got three more wickets in the second innings, but we lost that one. Then in Adelaide I scored 30 not out, batting number 11, and took four wickets in the second knock. But we lost that too.

I didn't have much success in the next three Shield matches, but there was a big surprise in store for me around Christmas time. My uncle had had a heart attack, and I took Mum to see him in hospital. We got back fairly late at night, and there was a car in the driveway. It belonged to Tony Radanovic, one of the Bankstown players.

Tony said, 'I'm not saying a word. Trust me. I want you to come down the club with me. There's a few blokes want to have a drink.'

I said, 'It's a bit late, isn't it?' But Mum said, 'Go on. You might as well.'

All the boys were there, all the Bankstown grade side. They must have been looking for me. But I'd been at the hospital. They wasted no time in telling me I'd been picked to play for Australia against Pakistan. It was the biggest shock of my life. I was on top of the world.

There was just one little problem, that soon became a big one. During one of the Shield matches at Sydney — I forget actually which one — I'd hurt my left foot. I bowled a short ball and the foot hit flat on the pitch. You know how you know straightaway that you've hurt something? It was bloody sore. I could hardly walk on it. It was a big decision, whether to let on about it. I mean, if I'd pulled out, I might never have been picked for Australia again. I made the wrong decision.

I just couldn't bowl properly. I kept falling away to the left, and the ball immediately went to the right. It was a dead wicket too. Six centuries were scored on it, four by Australia, two by Pakistan. I took none for 100. I bowled one session pretty well, but then the foot just gave out on me. I couldn't even walk back to the Hotel Windsor from the ground after the game.

Back in Sydney I had the foot X-rayed, and the doctor told me there was a broken bone. 'The only way you can fix it up,' he said, 'is just to rest it. You can't play for the rest of this season.'

Okay, so next summer I was ready to make up for it. I trained and built myself up. I'd show 'em what I could do, because I'd let a lot of people down — or at least I'd let myself down. Now I went to Shield practices, and I was bowling quick, beautifully, you name it, bowling everybody out. But the day the first New South Wales side was picked, Kerry O'Keeffe came up to me and said, 'Bad luck, Thommo.'

I said, 'What?' He said, 'Don't you know?' I said, 'No. What?' He said, 'Oh, it doesn't matter.'

The selectors weren't even big enough to come up to me and say I was dropped. My last game had been a Test; I was good enough to play for Australia then. I'd been told by a medical adviser to rest. Now I didn't even make the Shield side! That was a great old how-d'ya-do.

That's when it really started in grade cricket! I went home as disappointed as hell, but when I cooled down I said to myself, 'Right! That's it! Now it's on for young and old!'

And that season there were arms, legs, heads, wickets — you name it — flying everywhere! I didn't care what got in the way as I hurled the ball down in fury. Blokes just didn't want to face me. It was simple as that. I took about 45 wickets for Bankstown pretty cheaply and Greg Bush of Mosman wasn't the only fella I sent to hospital.

The selectors just had to look at me again, and eventually I was picked to play against Queensland in the final match of the season, in Sydney. If they beat New South Wales they would have won the Sheffield Shield for the first time ever. They had a surprise coming.

Young Thommo gave 'em the fastest bowling of the season, a right old touch-up. I got 7 for 85, including Sam Trimble, Greg Chappell (caught behind down the leg side), and Phil Carlson. Brian Taber said he had to stand yards further back keeping wicket than he'd ever had to stand before.

Between this game and the start of the next season, 1974-75, I got an offer to transfer to Queensland. They said they'd guarantee me a game and employment with radio station 4IP. The offer came just at the right time.

Perhaps I'd better say what I'd been doing with myself since I left school at eighteen. First I used to work as a wharfie down at Darling Harbour, loading wool bales and beer barrels. I used to load a couple of hundred 18-gallon kegs in a day, picking up a full one on my own — bang — just like that. As for wool bales, I could roll them around on my ear. I was never so fit.

Then I got a job in the Commonwealth Bank. For a year and a half I was at the Wiley Park branch, and I might as well break off here to tell about the day we were held up, robbed.

It was a Wednesday, and I'd just come off the counter. It was a small branch — just four guys and a manager. It was run superbly. We'd open at ten and close at three and balance and everything by half-past. I was a teller and I'd do a load of other things as well.

Anyway, this day of the hold-up, the second officer was checking everything, and I was just helping them out during my lunch hour so we could all nick off early later on. I had my back to the counter, and, Geez, something's wrong. You know how sometimes you can feel something's wrong? I thought things sounded quiet. Two blokes had slipped in unnoticed. They looked ordinary enough, dressed like any other customers in this area, which was sort of industrial. Only one of them had a sawn-off shotgun pointed at the teller, who was pooping himself! Poor bloke. Reminded me of 'Wizard' — you know, Ian Davis.

Geez, I thought. What's going on here? The other bloke's got a gun pointed at my mate next to me. For some reason or other they didn't seem to quite notice me. I thought, Right, I'll slip out the back door here and do something — ring up or something.

I got right to the door, and they didn't even notice me. I almost made it when one of the blokes saw me and swung his gun round. 'Ay you!' he says. 'Back! And get your hands up!'

'Don't shoot!' I shouted out. I had my hands in my pockets, and I didn't want them to think I was going for something.

One of them went into the manager's office then. The manager's sitting behind his desk reading the *Herald*. I remember when I started in the bank. He'd been in the war and he was a real stand-over major type from the army — you know the type: 'You, sonny, do everything by the book and we'll look after you. But just you step out of line . . .' That sort of treatment.

Anyway, he's got his glasses down on his nose, reading the paper, and when he hears this fella walk through the door with a gun on him, he looks over the top of his paper, and you've never seen a bloke poop himself so much in your life! It was kind of hilarious, and I couldn't help laughing, even in this crisis.

The manager was so flaming nervous after they'd gone that he couldn't sign his name. Nor could the second-in-charge. They could hardly talk! We had to do that for him! There he was shaking, yet the other junior and myself had been giving the robbers lip. When they told my mate to lift the safe up, he said, 'I ain't gonna lift that. What d'you think I am, bloody Superman? How d'you expect me to lift that bloody great thing up?' And the robbers were really getting nervous. They reckoned we were stalling them, and they kept looking over their shoulder.

But you should have seen the bank manager. Geez, it was funny. He was absolutely pooping himself!

They ended up catching the robbers, up at Palm Beach I think it was, not then but later on. I forget how much they took from our bank. They'd knocked over a few banks in Sydney.

I got some merit awards and good reports from the bank during my short career, but what ended it was when they transferred me to the Wentworth Hotel branch in town. I'd told them I never wanted to work in the big office in town. I preferred the suburbs, because of the cricket. The bank usually always backs you up when it comes to sport.

That was the downfall of my banking career. It was a drag. It was shift-work and I had to get into town every day, so after a few months I gave it away. I was now unemployed, just playing cricket and living off what I got from Sheffield Shield matches.

I was still living with my parents, and then I got a job at Monier Concrete, where Dad was a gatekeeper, out at Villawood. I was in the office as a clerk, with prospects of becoming a public relations rep. After a few months in the office I was made a sales rep. That was a great job, plenty of wining and dining architects, engineers and all that caper. Drinking plenty of grog. But it was upsetting my cricket, so one day I walked in to see the sales manager, and I said, 'Fred, look, this is no good to me. I can't drink, and I can't do the job properly. I want to get back to play Test cricket. The only way I'm going to do that is put in a big effort. No drinking. None of these late hours running around. I want to make it.'

So I finished up, but we ended still all good mates and my old man still works there. But I was unemployed again. I didn't go on the dole; I've never taken unemployment money in my life. I threw myself into my cricket, and that's the season I really went beserk in grade cricket, and they gave me that game against Queensland. Then came the Queensland offer.

Just before the 1974-75 season began I moved up to Brisbane. It was quite a lonely feeling at first. It was a big step, because I'd hardly even been away from home. I was a real family sort of kid. I remember looking out of the window of the plane and thinking, 'Hell! But I've got to do it.' As it turned out, I never looked back.

I started work in Brisbane as a car salesman. I sold a few, but it wasn't really a go either. I used to spend heaps of time at cricket practice. I'd be down at the Gabba practising with Sam Trimble, and I had to give the job away eventually, because I'd got it into my mind that I was going to absolutely slay 'em. There was no two ways about it.

Part of the trouble was that the situation wasn't exactly the way it was promised. They were going to give me this, give me that — all roses. I was supposed to have a job with an electronics firm and accommodation thrown in. It all turned out to be bullswool, and I ended up as a bloody car salesman.

Just before I'd left Sydney there was a big article about me in a cricket magazine that said I was a brutal killer and all that caper. A lot of it was blown up out of proportion, but it didn't do me any harm. Any publicity is good publicity, and though it wasn't true to say that I enjoyed seeing batsmen twitching on the ground and bleeding all over the place after I'd hit 'em, it probably didn't do my image any harm. Fellows who'd played against me knew what I was like, and the Poms soon found out.

CHAPTER 4

Gideon and Foulfellow

The England team that landed in Australia late in 1974, led by Mike Denness, can have had little idea of the ordeal awaiting them at the hands of Australia's fast bowlers. One, Dennis Lillee, had fought his way back to fitness after three stress fractures of the lower spine, and the other, Jeff Thomson, was barely heard of outside Australia's shores. Some of the claims made on his behalf — his blinding speed, his hard-to-pick-up bowling action, his lust for batsmen's blood — had filtered into England, but were dismissed as typical Australian pre-tour terror propaganda.

England had fought their way to a drawn series in West Indies a year earlier and then trampled all over India in three Tests. A drawn three-Test series against the visiting Pakistan side had seen Denness and his men off to Australia in confident mood, open to criticism perhaps only in that John Snow had been left out. He would still have been a force, despite a loss of pace, on the grounds where he had dictated matters with Ray Illingworth's side four years earlier.

Still, England now had Bob Willis and Peter Lever, both pretty sharp, and Geoff Arnold, Chris Old, Mike Hendrick and Tony Greig. It seemed, even if Ian Chappell, in England on a reconnaissance mission, thought otherwise, that England would again control the fast-bowling war if there was one.

With no hint of what sensations lay ahead, Thommo had begun his club cricket in Brisbane with two expensive wickets for Toombul against University. Then, against Souths (with Greg Chappell), he bowled very fast and took 6 for 75 in 17 overs.

In his first match for Queensland he took six New South Wales wickets at Brisbane, again making batsmen and spectators take notice of his sheer speed. It was reported that if he could have been more accurate, he would have taken twice as many wickets. All his wickets were top batsmen, one of them, Doug Walters, losing his leg stump to a lightning inswinger.

There was an unusual hindrance to his performance, as Thommo recalls:

I've just remembered what a close shave I had at the start of that season. I suppose I might never have taken part in the Tests, because in the first Shield match, my debut for Queensland against my old State, New South Wales, I got sunstroke.

I just didn't like wearing hats, and it was a pretty warm day that day in Brisbane. I came off, feeling a bit daggy, a bit funny in the stomach, a bit tired. They called a doctor in and he rushed me off to hospital and they diagnosed it as sunstroke. They let me go, and I stayed at Greg Chappell's that night, but I couldn't move. I sat down, and I couldn't move my neck or anything. Fortunately it passed, but I sometimes wear a hat now when the tropical sun gets a bit bloody much.

With a satisfying nine-wicket victory behind them, Queensland next took on Western Australia, and although Thommo took only two wickets, they were top men — Inverarity and Ross Edwards. He was starting to come into Test selection talk.

Greg Chappell showed little of the 'secret weapon's' bowling when Queensland played MCC just before the opening Test match. Thommo trapped Amiss in both innings, but on the whole he didn't impress. The explosion came a week later.

He doesn't remember all that much about his first Test against England. Details drained fast from his memory — not surprising in a man who lives exclusively day to day. A historic encounter it may have been, but to the 24-year-old express bowler it was a more satisfying chance to wipe away the memory of that absurd debut Test two years earlier:

When I was chosen in the Test team again, to play against England in Brisbane, I remember saying to myself, Hell, I've worked so hard between the last time I played for Australia and this time, what if it went wrong? But this just flashed through my mind and it was gone. I never worried about it after that. That's the sort of person I am.

For Queensland against the Poms I bowled only a couple of overs flat-out, and got a couple of wickets. I was just having a look, and I was real happy at what I saw.

It was a great feeling, that first Test I ever played against England. The Gabba ground was packed. It was great to be there, and I was really confident this time. Against Pakistan two years ago I was raw, and I thought I was lucky to be there. This time I knew no other bloke was better than me.

It's a great asset if you know what a bloke bats like, and I didn't know any of these Pommies. But I was sure I'd get a few of 'em out. The first dig was trial and error, but I'd got to know some of 'em in the second. I got two or three in the first and six or seven in the second.

To be exact, he took 3 for 69 in the first innings and 6 for 46 off 17.5 overs in the second. Every one of them was a Test centurymaker except for Hendrick, and none of them could 'read' him comfortably.

He first got the feel of the match by making 23, coming in last, and adding a precious 52 with Max Walker for the tenth wicket. Then, after lunch on the second day, watched by Lindwall and Miller from the Press-box, Lillee and Thomson began to write one of cricket history's most dramatic chapters. Running in as the crowd fell hushed, they took it in turns to torture the English batsmen with electrifying bouncers, yorkers, lifters from a length. Keith Miller later wrote that Thommo 'even frightened me sitting 200 yards away', and thought he made Lillee seem to be only in second gear.

Thomson made one kick venomously at Luckhurst, and Marsh made a fine catch. John Edrich was immediately ducking for dear life. Soon Dennis Amiss was caught at gully off a brute of a ball that cut in at his chest off a length. Thommo's first ball to Denness, the England captain, screamed past head-high, and the rattled batsman was soon a victim of Walker's. Fletcher played on to Lillee, and at the close England were four down for 114 after the phlegmatic Edrich and the counter-attacking Tony Greig had doubled the disastrous score.

Next day Thommo took his third wicket when Edrich fended a lifter to Ian Chappell at slip, and it soon developed into a nightmare match for England as the unpredictable bounce produced catches that always seemed to be held by the close fielders, irrespective of degree of difficulty.

Greig's century was bold, cheeky, and one of the best in the long history of England-Australia Tests. But though it shortened the first-innings deficit to 44 runs, Australia worked their way to 5 for 288 before the declaration on the fourth evening, Greg Chappell, Edwards, Walters and Marsh all making runs. England would have had just on forty minutes to withstand the Australian demons that evening, but the motorised roller broke down, and Alderman Clem Jones managed to give the pitch only half the allowable seven minutes' rolling. The delay, added to bad light, meant that Amiss and Luckhurst had to face only two overs. Still, Thommo and Lillee bowled murderously, and the Englishmen were grateful to have stumps drawn when they were.

On the last day of that bellicose Test match at Brisbane, England were shot out for 166, giving Australia a win by exactly that margin of runs. Lillee struck first, getting Luckhurst, and then Thommo bowled the usually impregnable Edrich, who was nursing a broken right hand. He greeted Denness with one that smacked him on the shoulder. Before lunch Thommo picked up his second wicket when he had Amiss (batting with a broken thumb — courtesy of Thommo) caught by Walters at third slip off another lifter that struck the bat handle. And after the interval it became a complete rout.

Denness was dazzlingly caught at slip by Walters, and Greig was no problem this time. Thommo flung down a near-invisible yorker and the blond giant was bowled before he could start to bring his bat down. By now it was attack, attack by Australia. England weren't going to get the runs, and Ian Chappell piled his men into the catching positions, leaving the field in front of the batsmen virtually deserted.

Peter Lever, whose inclination to bowl short had won him no admirers locally, now fended off a Lillee lifter and was almost relieved, it seemed, to be caught at short leg.

Thommo added the scalps of the patient Alan Knott and — to finish the match — Hendrick, and all his frustrations of past seasons were washed away, his ambitions to command the course of a Test match realised.

There were many observers, including some of the England players, who thought that he owed much to the pitch, which was plainly under-prepared, and that he would be manageable on the fast but true track at Perth. But the mental and physical bruises had to heal first, and there really was no guarantee that the new Lillee-Thomson menace, backed up by such superlative catching, would fade as the series progressed.

Across Australia excitement spread at the knowledge that a new destroyer had arrived. 'Typhoon' they called him, ignoring any patent on the word that Frank Tyson might have incorporated twenty years earlier. 'Tornado' — a little nearer original. 'Terror' — this one had yet to be accepted generally, for surely, some thought, no newcomer could expect to go on doing this sort of thing on a true Test match wicket?

Meanwhile, back in England, following an emergency call for a reinforcement batsman, 42-year-old Colin Cowdrey was preparing to fly out to Australia, to add a calmness and a solid technique to a tottering side. All he — and the rest of the British public — had seen of Jeff Thomson was the exaggeratedly hostile events of a half-hour highlights segment on television each frosty evening. There, on the small screen, in vivid sub-tropical colours contrasting greatly with the drabness of early English winter, and to the accompaniment of a ceaseless howl of approval from the drooling crowd, the Australian fast bowlers seemed to be claiming a wicket with every ball, when they weren't inflicting horrible injury or clipping cap-peaks with their bouncers. A gruesome preview for a cosily-built veteran as he made the brave decision to join MCC in Perth.

When Thommo heard he was coming, he said, 'He'll cop it as quick as anyone!'

Thommo was now hot property. In only his twelfth first-class game he had established worldwide fame — some said notoriety. 'I'm no gorilla,' he told the Press. 'I'm a pretty quiet sort of a bloke really.'

There were times, though, when he wasn't so quiet. One of the most distinguished and lordly English cricket correspondents effected an introduction to him at a reception later in the series and received for his trouble an acid 'Are you one of those Pommie --------s who've been writing all that ---- about me?' Exit one startled journalist.

The English public as well as the touring party — players,

management, writers, holidaymakers — were seized by varying waves
of alarm. The destruction of their batsmen had a familiar and
frightening, not to say depressing, ring about it, resurrecting gruesome
thoughts of Griffith and Hall, or, further back, Miller and Lindwall —
a kind of Bodyline received and not dispensed.

In time, of course, Dennis Lillee emerged as the real hard man. Jeff
Thomson was adequately summed up by someone who knew a thing or
two about quick bowling, Frank Tyson: 'Thomson is a natural
phenomenon that the resilient background of Australian cricket throws
up from time to time. He is, however, the happy warrior, the person
every real fast bowler should be.'

Almost spot on.

Thommo's success in the Brisbane Test had been based on shortish
spells, often into the stiff breeze, sometimes uncharacteristically
accurate, sometimes all over the place, making Rod Marsh's job
impossible behind the stumps. His outswinger often went like a
boomerang, but when the line was wrong it looked very bad.

By the three-quarter mark of the series, Marsh was desperate to get
some time off, so badly bruised were his hands. He had already
awarded the prize for speed to Thommo — who could judge better? —
though he felt Lillee was a yard faster in 1972 than during this '74-75
series. The Englishmen considered them both fast enough.

Colin Cowdrey's mission was to stay at the crease and draw the fire
from the Australian terror twins. Patience and nerve were the qualities
called for, and the veteran of 109 Test matches stepped off the aircraft
almost four years since last having played for England and a mere four
days before treading gently but determinedly back into the fiery arena
at Perth.

Luckhurst was the first to go, caught off Walker for 27 after Ian
Chappell had put England in to bat. Cowdrey then bravely did the job
he was sent out to do. He moved in front of his stumps, sometimes
swaying from the bucking ball, sometimes meeting it with a perfectly
straight bat. Runs seemed far from his mind. After twenty minutes he
got his first.

After lunch the partnership between left-hand opener David
Lloyd, who was taking occasional punishment, and Cowdrey, who was
weathering well, advanced the total to 99. Cowdrey had introduced
himself to Thommo during the break for drinks, shaking his hand
almost affectionately and perhaps bewildering the young adversary.
Soon, though, the knockout blow was to be delivered.

First, Lloyd went, cutting at Thomson but getting only a fine edge
which Greg Chappell somehow clung to at second slip, one-handed. As
so often, Thommo looked an even greater danger with a slightly worn
ball, after a fairly wayward opening spell.

The Cowdrey shuffle then brought about his downfall. He went too
far across against Thommo and had his leg stump disturbed. The

breakthrough had been made, and England collapsed from that point, only Knott resisting for long with 51. Some amazing catches were taken — two more by Greg Chappell, on his way to breaking the world Test record for a non-wicketkeeper of six catches (his grandfather, Vic Richardson, being one of the previous holders). Ashley Mallett and Ian Redpath also took brilliant catches, and Walters threw out Geoff Arnold from the deep.

These were the features Thommo was to remember when the Australian side was bereft of its stars of the mid-1970s at the time of the World Series defections. This was the stuff of which memories were made, an attachment and a comradeship that meant as much to Ian Chappell's players as companionship in combat ever meant to troops at the front.

Australia now piled it on. On the second day they hit 351 runs for the loss of four wickets, Doug Walters smacking Willis for six off the final ball to reach 103. Ross Edwards went on to reach his century on the third day, and then it was time for England to climb back on the rack, 273 runs behind on the first innings.

With Luckhurst nursing an injured hand, Cowdrey opened with Lloyd, who, on 17 after nearly two hours, took a sickening blow low down from Thommo and had to retire. Soon afterwards Cowdrey was leg-before to Thommo for 41, again having batted for over two hours; but that was the extent of Australia's drive that day.

On the fourth morning, though, England were back in the horrors. Beginning at 102 for the loss of Cowdrey, they collapsed to Thommo, who started with Greig, caught high at slip, then had Denness and Fletcher with consecutive balls, the England captain at gully and the slight Essex batsman taken by Marsh off a near-unplayable ball.

Thommo's fellow-assassins chipped in as the day progressed, Fred Titmus, another 42-year-old, resisting stoutly for 61 and Chris Old hammering 43. Thommo caught Old, running some distance to collect a skyer. Then he bowled Arnold to record his fifth wicket of the innings, and soon England were out for 293, leaving Australia to make 21 for victory and a two-nil lead in the series. This they duly did, with over a day's scheduled play remaining.

Australia was a happy land, and seven-wicket Thommo was one of the main heroes, well on his way now to becoming the subject of newspaper cartoons ('Ashes to Ashes, dust to dust; if Thomson don't get ya, Lillee must'), jingles ('We got Thommo'), illustrations on T-shirts, pub talk, and the adulation of kids as well as their mums and dads — and elder sisters.

After the Shield match in Perth, he lined up for Australia again for the third Test, at Melbourne, a match which began on Boxing Day and ended on New Year's Eve with neither side quite bold enough to go for victory. With almost 43,000 people awaiting a third Australian victory in a row in the series, the batsmen dithered. Needing 75 runs in 105 minutes, Rod Marsh and Max Walker played very cautiously, Marsh in particular seeming to resent England's defensive bowling and field placing. Seven runs came from seven overs from Titmus and Underwood, and then Denness took the new ball, and Marsh, Walker and Lillee turned on the power.

Then, with three overs left and 16 runs needed, only two came from the first of them and Underwood bowled a maiden next over to Lillee. With 14 needed of the last, bowled by Tony Greig, Australia lost Lillee, which brought in Mallett, and finished the match eight runs short of victory with two wickets in hand.

It would have been interesting to have had Thommo in for those last three overs. Chances are he would have done something to evoke frenzied cheers from the crowd; instead of which, there were disillusioned catcalls.

On this slow Melbourne wicket Thommo had done well to take four wickets in each innings, six of the eight being top batsmen. This took his tally for the series to 24, and already the record-conscious were looking to Arthur Mailey's long-standing record of 36 wickets for Australia in a Test series against England. Thommo seemed well in line to knock it over, especially as six Tests were scheduled.

He did more than bag another large swag of Pom wickets in this game. He incurred the umpire's wrath by bowling too much short stuff — as did Dennis Lillee — and dealt a near-crippling blow to the right knee of Fred Titmus, who somehow gathered himself up and continued, and later bowled in some discomfort.

Bowling usually into the breeze, in front of a huge crowd — almost 80,000 — Thommo had got rid of David Lloyd with a nasty kicker that hit the glove, and soon his bounce was too much even for 'Bacchus' Marsh, whose leap left him short of the careering ball. His next wicket was that of Cowdrey, leg-before. And then came a scare as he pulled up with hamstring trouble, shortly after the flailing Tony Greig had nicked a flyer to Greg Chappell at slip, only to see the chance go down. Thommo's trouble started when he flung out a foot to stop a ball played back along the wicket, and he didn't show up again that day.

English relief was shortlived, however, for he came out at the start of the second day — against the advice of the physiotherapist, who told him to rest if he felt any twinges at the nets. The old Thommo 'gimme-a-walking-stick-or-something-I-wanna-get-at-'em' attitude.

Gradually he built his speed up, and added the wickets of Willis, caught at cover, and Knott, intelligently bowled by a yorker as he tried to improvise by moving out to leg to hit through the off side.

Australia finished one run short of England's 242, and it was anyone's match, a change from the lopsided first two Tests. Bad light spared Amiss and Lloyd the horrible prospect of 25 minutes against Lillee and Thomson that evening.

After the rest day Thommo bowled a rare over to get things under way again: three bouncers and one near-bouncer, some wild inswingers, and a wide. He tried like mad, but the England openers gutsed it out, and it was not until they had made 115 for the first wicket — easily their best start of the series — that Lloyd went, caught-and-bowled by Mallett.

Thommo's first wicket in the second innings came when he got the tough little left-hander, John Edrich, for the third time in four Test innings, caught by Marsh after being surprised by the lift of the ball. And straight after drinks, he found the edge of Denness's bat as the captain moved to leg, and Ian Chappell scooped the catch up at slip.

After Dennis Amiss's gallant 90 came to an end, to another catch by the Australian captain, off Mallett, Thommo chipped in again with Knott's wicket, caught behind. And before he took a spell he dealt Titmus the paralysing blow to the inside of the knee.

When he came back, Greig having departed for a very valuable and animated 60, Thommo finished the innings off by bowling Willis, giving himself figures of 8 for 143 in the match and helping to set up the chance of yet another win. By the following evening Chappell's champions were glad to slip quietly home for a draw.

After the one-day international, which England won by three wickets, the sides moved on to Sydney for the fourth Test, and this is where the Ashes were won, four years after Ray Illingworth's England team had taken them from Australia on the same ground.

After mounting pressure, Mike Denness, with 65 runs in six Test innings, dropped himself from the England XI, and John Edrich took over the leadership. Two factors — that Australia won with 5.3 overs to spare, and that Edrich came back to the crease after getting two ribs cracked by Lillee and managed to hold on to the end, not out 33 — were significant. But for that lethal ball, even though it didn't take a wicket, England would probably have forced a draw. As in the previous Test, it was a king-sized 'if'.

Australia won the toss and batted this time, raising a healthy total of 405 that owed its tailend kick to a stand of 37 between Ashley Mallett, 31, and Thommo, who hit 24 not out, and fine innings by Rick McCosker, 80 in his Test debut, and Greg Chappell, 84.

Then it was on again, to the delight of the mob on the Hill. Lillee took the Randwick end, and Thommo purred in from the Paddington end. His first over was comic. He began with a wide and followed with two uncontrolled bouncers which flew for four byes apiece, one soaring over the heads of batsman and wicketkeeper, the other veering way down the leg side, leaving Marsh spreadeagled on the ground, like a beaten goalkeeper. After three overs, Thommo, out of rhythm, was off.

Not until after lunch did he make any further impression. Then, he made a good short-leg catch to get rid of Lloyd off Lillee's bowling, and soon after, having beaten Cowdrey with pace twice running, he had him caught at short leg. By stumps, England were 3 for 106, still 299 runs behind.

One of the very few Australian dropped catches marked the start of the third day, Ian Chappell missing a hard one off Edrich from

Thomson's bowling. But Redpath soon made up for it, holding a dazzling left-handed catch at leg slip to finish Fletcher off from Walker's bowling. Then came the prize wicket of Tony Greig — prize because all through the series he was the one England batsman to 'take on' the fearsome Aussie fast attack. Swishing defiantly at the flying ball, crunching it through the covers when it was pitched up (a rarity), and signalling his own boundaries to draw flames to Lillee's eyes, he was the symbol of arrogance and refusal to knuckle under. He exchanged language with bowlers and fielders, and just as often as he enraged them to more miles-per-hour he put them off their stroke.

This time, though, his luck was out (and luck was such a necessary ingredient for batsmen facing this relentless blitzkrieg). He played forward to a Thommo outswinger, and Greg Chappell did the rest at second slip. England 5 for 123.

Alan Knott had a charmed life. He immediately edged Thommo and was incredibly missed by Marsh. Then there was a loud shout for caught-behind, and the umpire saw in the batsman's favour. Thommo's next ball, a late indipper, all but bowled the little Englishman. The boy from Bankstown was rested after five overs, having taken one for 12, with two dropped catches.

Walters chipped in during the afternoon with the wickets of acting captain Edrich (50) and Titmus, but with the advent of the new ball the English counter-attack, led by Knott (82), ended. The plucky little 'keeper drew away again to cut Thomson, but the bowler let rip a leg-stump yorker, and that was that. A while later he did the same to Willis, to finish off the innings for 295, his own figures 4 for 74.

Thommo seemed to the Englishmen to be getting better and better, faster and faster, virtually unhookable when he dropped short, and too quick when he got his yorker right. There was Knott, taking guard deep inside the crease, saying after the tour was over that his theory was that every inch counted. Considering the micro-second it took the ball to travel an inch, or even a yard, it really wouldn't have seemed to matter.

Ian Redpath and Greg Chappell made centuries in Australia's second innings, Chappell's typically graceful and watchable, and Australia declared on the fourth afternoon, leaving England eight-and-a-half hours to get 400. It might as well have been 800, but the time factor remained of interest, especially when an hour and a half was lost immediately to bad light and a rain squall. When they eventually started, chances were missed off both Thomson and Lillee, and England survived to be 33 without loss.

The anticipated collapse came on the last day, though the action was stretched into the last half-hour. Three wickets went while England advanced to 74, and at that total Edrich took the blow in the ribs and went to hospital for X-rays. The crowd, bloodthirsty as ever, carried on its 'Lill-ee, Lill-ee' chant while the England cricket-writers and many of the players themselves wondered where it would all end.

The 42-year-old and infamous word 'Bodyline' entered conversation as seldom before, and the old-time Australian Test player 'Stork' Hendry came straight out and said it: the methods Australia's fast bowlers were employing were, he felt, *worse* than those of Larwood and Voce in the 1932-33 series, and he took it upon himself to apologise to English cricket-lovers for Australia's 'non-cricket' tactics.

He would not have enjoyed Keith Fletcher's dismissal. Thommo pounded the ball in only fractionally short of a length, and up it spat, cracking the batsman on the edge of his cap via the bat-handle and almost giving Ross Edwards at cover a catch. It as good as finished Fletcher. Thommo sensed his opponent's unnerved state and rasped in a fast ball well up. Fletcher, even more inclined than the rest of his side to go onto the back foot, poked out hurriedly and speared a catch to Redpath at gully.

English wickets continued to topple, some of them apparently needlessly against the slower bowling that came as a relief to the shellshocked batsmen. Knott didn't like his bat-pad catch, and Titmus top-edged a sweep, also off Mallett, to be caught by Thomson at square leg. Shortly Greig charged at Mallett and was stumped, and by tea, with the courageous Edrich back at the crease with Willis, England were 8 for 184.

It dragged on afterwards, thanks to Edrich's farming of the strike and skilful handling of all that Australia could pile on him. Then, at last, Mallett had Geoff Arnold caught in close by Greg Chappell — his thirteenth catch of the series and Ashley Mallett's hundredth Test wicket — and Australia had won the Ashes. They were jubilant, and they showed it.

A record Sydney crowd over the five days of 178,027 had watched the contest, and although the umpires had warned the fast bowlers of both sides for intimidation, especially at tailend batsmen, and although there had been a good deal of bitterness in the match, it had had its moments. There was McCosker's fine debut (spoilt somewhat t y a blow on the head while fielding); Greg Chappell's two magnificent innings; Alan Knott's cheekiness and John Edrich's courage; and six more wickets for Thommo, who now had 30 in the series and had smartly squashed any last vestiges of suspicion that he was a flash in the pan.

It was a very quaint fact that Dennis Lillee had taken two wickets in each and every England innings in the series so far, giving him 16. Opinion was divided as to whether his being upstaged by new-boy Thomson contributed to his excessive aggression — not only with the ball but with his tongue. There was no doubt that he meant it when he tore into a batsman after he had played and missed or got an edge. There was no doubt that he went much further through on his followthrough than his momentum called for, and that, when he was face to face with the quizzical batsman, he meant what he said. And it wasn't all that nice.

This was the school bully, at odds with the world. At the other end, his face hair-free, his mouth always ready to spread into a grin, was his accomplice, a fellow who loved taking wickets and winning matches but who could just as easily be persuaded to go water-skiing or fishing. Hatred was, if not unknown to him, a very distant propellant.

About this time the BBC flew out a crew to do a filmed interview with Australia's Masters of Terror, and the relationship between the fast bowlers was clearly shown. Lillee did most of the talking — serious, intense stuff, with the machismo touch. Jeff Thomson was the light relief. The subject of drinking after the game with the opposition came up. 'Yeah,' said Thommo, in that increasingly recognisable squawk of his, 'I'd drink with 'em. Trouble is, ya can never find any Poms to drink with, eh Dennis?'

He reminded me so much of Gideon, the sidekick to J. Worthington Foulfellow ('Honest John') in Walt Disney's *Pinocchio*. There were even times when you could practically hear D.K. Lillee singing 'Hi diddly dee, an actor's life for me. . . .'

Not that the scenario was anything but a sombre melodrama for the Englishmen by now. Nursing all kinds of injuries to their hands and bodies, as well as to their pride, some also had their nerves afflicted by the almost ceaseless bombardment. Mike Denness gave an insight into the shattering effect of Australia's attack on some of his batsmen when he wrote of David Lloyd in his book *I Declare* (something, incidentally, that he was never remotely in a position to do — declare, that is — until the final Test, when the Lillee-Thomson threat was removed for the time being):

'When David Lloyd came back into the dressing-room after his dismissal, as I was padding up, I said, "Well played, David." He replied, "Bloody hell, captain, you never get any balls in your own half." Any cricketer getting out in a Test match, or any other game, is obviously annoyed with himself. He may come in and throw his bat down or just sit in silence, inwardly cursing himself for getting out. But, on this occasion, within seconds of his dismissal the whole of Lloyd's body was quivering. His neck and the top half of his body, in particular, were shaking. He was shellshocked, suffering from the effects of never having to move around so quickly in all his life. It was the reaction from his continual ducking and weaving to get out of the firing line.'

This took place during the third Test, at Melbourne. There were still bad times ahead. It was David Lloyd, the jokey Lancashire left-hander, who was supposed to have written home to his mother the remark: 'Dear Mum, Today I got a half-volley bowled at me — in the nets. And I didn't know what to do with it!'

Adelaide, during the fifth Test match, was where Thommo was expected to smash Mailey's 36-wicket record, and after Australia's batting difficulties on a drying pitch (they recovered from 5 for 84 to

304 all out, Underwood 7 for 113 and Terry Jenner top-scoring with 74), Thommo was among the wickets again.

They didn't come instantly, for his opening spell, into the wind, seemed lethargic. Lillee, downwind as usual, bowled faster this day, and was to come away from Adelaide with eight wickets, double his ration so far, and fairer reward for his magnificent skills and stamina.

When he came on later with the wind at his back, with legions of slips fielders and short legs, Thommo got Cowdrey again, out to an Aussie Rules-type catch by Max Walker at square leg. Denness followed, having made 51. He moved back from a Thomson flyer and the ball flicked the top edge of the bat and provided Marsh with yet another catch.

He came back for another bowl later in the afternoon, after the Englishmen had done some desperate things against the slower bowling in their relief at getting away from the speed and bounce for a while, and after having Fletcher dropped, Thommo had him caught at slip by Ian Chappell for 40.

It was his 33rd wicket of the series — a staggering performance — and yet it was to be his last. On the rest day he damaged his shoulder, and that put him out of the match and out of the sixth Test as well.

He remembers quite clearly how it came about:

Adelaide's brought me quite a bit of bad luck. The first of several injuries there was when I did my shoulder playing tennis up at Yalumba, up in the Barossa Valley, at Wyndie Hill Smith's place. It was the rest day of the Test against the Poms, and it was so many years since I'd played tennis. They've got this grass court next to the swimming pool, and I'm playing with Neil Kerley, the South Australian footballer, Doug Walters and Brian Taber. I served the ball hard, as I usually do, and felt a terrible pain in my shoulder. It just went.

I dropped the racquet and went straight to a specialist, who diagnosed a pulled tendon and torn muscles. The irony of the whole thing was that I served an ace, which made me feel a lot better.

It was a bit of a pity because I had 33 wickets up to then, and I probably would've passed Arthur Mailey's record for Australia against England, something that Rodney Hogg eventually did in the 1978-79 series.

Hoggy's quick, but not that quick. He makes you play at him most of the time — bowls a good off-cutter. But there weren't many blokes in the Pommie team you could call batsmen. I reckon I would've got wickets bowling left-handed! Randall and Gower can bat a bit, but Boycott's past it. He didn't bat anything like he batted against us in England in 1977. Of course, I missed him — or should I say he missed me — when I was bowling all systems go in 1974 and '75. No, Hoggy bowled okay, but he didn't have such a top bowler at the other end as I had in Dennis Lillee. That helps you in one way, but it means somebody else is likely to be getting among the wickets all the time too.

As I said, Adelaide's been bad news for me several times. In the Pakistan Test I got a shocking shoulder injury, which I'll go into later. Then, in the 1978 Test against the Indians at Adelaide, bugger me if I don't go and get injured again. This time it was a muscle near the hamstring in my leg. I'd got two of them out for next to nothing. I was starting to bowl really quick, and getting a lot of bounce. Gavaskar was caught in the gully off the shoulder of his bat and Amarnath was caught at short leg off another lifter. Then I was walking back to my mark when — bang! I couldn't walk properly. It meant I missed the rest of the match, though I batted in our second innings. I think anybody would agree that if I'd been able to bowl in the last knock India wouldn't have got so near to getting the 500 or so they needed for victory.

Australia won quite comfortably without any further Thomson firepower. Alan Knott made a century, but Dennis Lillee put in another grand effort, and Australia went 4-0 up after five Tests.

Unexpectedly, England were free of the Lillee-Thomson menace altogether after just six overs by Lillee in that sixth Test at Melbourne. He was unable to continue because of an extremely painful pinched nerve in his instep. The contest was transformed.

Having got Australia out for a mere 152 (Peter Lever 6 for 38) on a pitch made treacherous by a damp patch, England then proceeded to pile up 529 runs, the captain, Mike Denness, making compensation for his previous agonies with an innings of 188, and Keith Fletcher doing the same with 146. Eighty-nine for Greig and 70 for Edrich, and the Englishmen were smiling again. All except Dennis Amiss, who managed to bag his third successive duck at the hands of Lillee just before the fast bowler was forced to retire.

In the entire series to date England had managed only one century stand. Now, with the 'terror twins' gone, they posted 149 for the third wicket, 192 for the fourth, and 148 for the fifth. Max Walker took the bowling honours now, after having given such wonderful support to Lillee and Thomson throughout the series. The large, cheerful Tasmanian turned Victorian took 8 for 143 off 42.2 overs.

So England saved the whitewash, winning by an innings, and were more than a little glad to be on their way. They were tired of the one-sided warfare and of the ignominy that went with it; tired of the constant advice coming from every quarter; tired of the caterwauling that came at them from the outer, where the drunken and semi-drunken Ockers took a fiendish delight in the Poms' discomfort and humiliation.

England knew two things for certain now: Dennis Lillee's back injury was fully repaired; and Jeff Thomson was all the forecasters said he would be — and more.

CHAPTER 5

Ambassador to Sri Lanka

A clue to the amazing powers of physical recovery of Jeff Thomson came five weeks after his Adelaide tennis injury. That weightlifter's shoulder had mended sufficiently for him to blast holes in Victoria's batting at Brisbane in a crucial Sheffield Shield encounter that left Western Australia as champions. Victoria, needing 18 points from the match, lost by ten wickets, and Thommo, having started with 3 for 89, made his highest first-class score, 61, and then skittled the Vics with 6 for 17.

Les Stillman, Graham Yallop and Trevor Laughlin were his first-innings victims in a total of 6 for 325 declared. Then Sam Trimble (77) and Greg Chappell (122) took Queensland to 203 before the second wicket fell. There was a mid-innings slump, and then Thommo strode forth and batted for two-and-a-quarter hours, the high-spot being four consecutive fours in an over from Max Walker — it would have been five, but the next drive crashed into the bowler's stumps.

On the third evening Victoria lost all hope as Thommo ran amok, taking four for six in 10 overs, with one sensational over when Ian Redpath fell to the first ball, Laughlin to the third, and Richie Robinson to the last. He was bowling his fastest of the summer — and that meant some speed. Victoria's all-out score of 76, their lowest in the Shield since 1927, was the end product. Thommo has always taken special satisfaction in taking Victorian wickets.

His analysis of 12.6 — 6 — 17 — 6 took his season's figures to 62 wickets at an average of 19.37, the same number of wickets as Lillee but at lower cost — by almost six runs each. Between them in the Tests they had taken 58 England wickets out of the 100 to fall to bowlers in the series while one or both of the terror twins was in action.

Their names were among the first written down by the Australian selectors as they chose their team to tour England, with Thommo needing only to pass a precautionary medical test. This he did on March 19, having withdrawn from the short Derrick Robins tour of South Africa. The only concession to the shoulder injury was more care in his returns to the wicketkeeper from the outfield. The bazooka throw was rarely seen now.

There were now fresh doubts that he would stay in Queensland. He told the Press that he'd had offers from other States and that he could be tempted to return to Bankstown. 'It's home, and it's where all the action is,' he said. Questioned about the possibility of growing tired of cricket, he replied: 'I've no worries about becoming mentally stale. The more cricket I play the more I like it.'

Shades of the lad who had to be bullied by his brother and mother into playing against St George rather than go fishing.

The real Thommo personality was beginning to emerge now, and the public gradually realised that he was not the spiteful piece of work he was made out to be by the notorious interview of eighteen months earlier and by subsequent conjectures. His Test skipper, Ian Chappell, made clear that Thommo's anger was severest when self-directed. In an article for *Cricketer*, the Melbourne magazine, Chappell wrote: 'When you talk to him on the field when he is bowling, all you hear is a stream of abuse aimed directly at himself for his terrible bowling. I have never known a guy who bowls so consistently badly in his own eyes, yet goes on getting bundles of wickets. He is exactly the same when he comes off the field after an innings — in fact, you wouldn't talk to your worst enemy the way he talks to himself.'

So, having enchanted a total paying audience of over three-quarters of a million at the grounds during the Tests against England, that deadly composite Australian lady 'Lillian Thomson' set off for the Old Country, Lillee to the scene of his heroic, record-breaking performances of 1972, Thomson for his first overseas tour.

They stopped over in Canada on the way, and managed to lose to Eastern Canada at Toronto. But Thommo took a hat-trick against British Columbia in the opening game, at Vancouver, and after a warm-up match at Lord's, for former England wicketkeeper John Murray's benefit, the Australians set about their World Cup campaign. Interest in the fast-bowling duo was at fever pitch, for the British public knew that here were the successors to the mighty Jack Gregory and Ted McDonald of 1921 and Ray Lindwall and Keith Miller of 1948. It seemed that phenomena like these happened every 27 years — which was quite often enough for English batsmen.

It was time, too, for some batsmen of other nations to sample the attack the whole world had been reading about for the past few months, and for the opening match, Australia v Pakistan, the gates at Headingley were closed, with 22,000 people inside awaiting the firework display. Lillee gave it to them, but Thommo was a bit of a fizzer.

Australia made 278 off their 60 overs, Thommo putting in a useful 20 not out at the end as Ross Edwards took his own score to 80 not out. Then the troubles began. In his first over Thommo was wild: five no-balls ('Umpire Tom Spencer was a bit bloody hard on me!'), one of which was also a wide and hurtled off to the boundary.

The crowd let him know what they thought of his debut performance, and he in turn let them know what he thought of them. He directed a jerky little two-finger gesture towards them — no way to silence a disdainful Yorkshireman. Or a Pressman, for that matter. A section of the British Press was waiting for this kind of reaction, and the Bankstown boy took some stick.

He also took the valuable wicket of Zaheer in his eight overs, with a final no-ball tally of a dozen; but the match was won by Lillee, who took 5 for 34 and won the Man of the Match award. That was a good start, and there was an expected walkover against Sri Lanka in the next match, at The Oval.

But first, there were net practices at Lord's, and there, a few days later, Thommo and his mates had some fun at the expense of their friends from the media. Egged on by some of the other players, Thommo deliberately overstepped the crease as he bowled, and the photographers and writers fell for it. His no-ball disease, some of them felt, was incurable. At last one of the terror twins was cut down to size.

Jock Livingston, the Australian-born left-hander who was such a prolific scorer for Northants in the 1950s, saw a lot of the Australians during the tour in his capacity of sales director for Gray-Nicolls, the bat manufacturers. He recalls that Jeff Thomson's cricket boots were almost falling apart — taped up with adhesive strapping. This almost certainly accounted for his erratic stride during the run-up, and it was Jock's idea to take tracings of Thommo's feet and send them to the old-established Northampton firm of Whitings to have perfect-fitting boots made. In due course these proved very helpful.

Meanwhile, Ian Chappell, the greatest of captains unto his men if not to all his opponents, hosts and Press, seeing the need to protect his young — even naive — quickie from any taunting and hostility, spelt out a clear message: 'Jeff's had a gutful of this business, and I don't want anyone talking to him about those no-balls.'

Soon, however, it was not no-balls with which he was associated. It was the old charge of brutality. The second-round match of the Prudential World Cup of 1975 was against one of the two Associate member countries, Sri Lanka, formerly Ceylon, the little island that bred a handful of fine batsmen and yearned for admission to Test cricket. This was their great chance to prove their worth on the hard and true Oval wicket after their mincing by West Indies in the first round. For a while things went well. Then Thommo did his thing:

That day at The Oval I'd managed to sort out the no-ball problem, and it was bad luck on the Sri Lankans that they were the opposition. It all clicked just right.

My team-mates, who were all really happy that I'd found my rhythm again, played a dirty trick on me here. They did me nicely. They knew I was keyed up and out to prove everything, a hundred per cent again. Anyway, I hit this bloke Mendis on the head. They're only little fellas, so you couldn't call it a bouncer exactly. He fell down face-first, and when they brought him around, his captain's saying 'You'll be right' or something or other. But Mendis just says, 'Oh my God! I'm going!' He went, and he wasn't coming back! They took him to hospital.

But the real trouble came when I hit Wettimuny on the foot. He was waltzing around, and he wanted to go too. That was enough for him. I'd already hit him in the chest. As I walked past him at the end of the over I said to him, 'Look, it's not broken, you weak bastard,' I said. 'I'll give you the tip,' I said, 'If you're down there next over it *will* be!

His captain gives him the pep talk, you know, stick around, I'll look after you, sort of caper. Then the captain obligingly just blocked out Dennis to make sure he wasn't going to get down my end! So this poor bastard was facing me again, and the ball landed in exactly the same spot and whacked him straight on the instep again. You should have seen him — jumping around, he was.

This is where the plot went into action. The ball had come straight back up the pitch to me, and as I collected it, the boys are yelling out, 'Throw down the stumps, Two-up, throw down the stumps!' I'm saying to myself, 'No, no, I can't do that, no' — all in a split-second. Then I thought 'Bugger it!' and I threw the ball and knocked the stumps over. I jumped up and shouted an appeal, but no other bastard's moved. They all sat or stood there with their arms folded! They'd done me stone cold on purpose!

It seemed The Oval was full of Indians and Sri Lankans, and they're all hooting and calling for my blood. The members were booing too.

All the World Cup teams were staying at the same hotel in Kensington, and I remember the next morning, when I came down for breakfast and to check for mail, I got out of the elevator to find all these Indians and Sri Lankans milling around in the foyer, some of them with bandages on their heads.

I thought, 'Geez, I'll get a knife in the back here for sure.' But the first bloke said, 'Mr Thomson, have you had breakfast yet?' I said, 'No' because I'd suddenly decided not to have breakfast. But it turned out they intended to be my best mates. They wanted to take me round to have breakfast with them. Perhaps they were trying to calm me down!

That game was getting to be a problem. We made 320-odd and then I got an early wicket, but Dennis and the others were just coasting along, and Sri Lanka were getting out of the bag. The runs were coming pretty easily, and that's when 'Bertie' came up to me and said, 'Have a bowl. I don't care what you do. Brain 'em, bowl 'em out, but whatever you do, we've got to win.' Ian Chappell was determined not to let this match get away from us. That's when the fun and games started.

Duleep Mendis (who, incidentally, vehemently denies saying 'God, I'm going') was very lucky — and so, for that matter, was Thommo. The ball struck the little Sri Lankan on the middle of the forehead, where the bone is thickest. Two inches either side, and that could have been it: the first fatality in big cricket since 1870.

Sunil Wettimuny, who left St Thomas's Hospital after treatment for severe bruising, gave his impressions of his own unhappy experience: 'After the first ball I felt shivers down my spine. Thomson seemed to be swearing and grinning at me at the same time.'

Chappell's sense of humour turned cruel-edge upwards at a Lord's Taverners dinner shortly afterwards when he introduced Jeff Thomson as 'our ambassador to Sri Lanka'. It all gave rise to speculation as to whether 'the ambassador' might have finished in jail, for the matter of sporting injuries and criminal responsibility was entering conversation more and more frequently now, especially since the near-fatal head injury to New Zealand's Ewen Chatfield at Auckland a few months previously. Hit by a deliberate bouncer from England's Peter Lever, the number eleven fell, twitching, turning purple in the face, and with his heart stopped for several seconds. Only the attention of the England team physio and a St John ambulanceman saved him.

When Mendis and Wettimuny were being attended to at the hospital, a policeman heard the exchange between one of the victims and a medical attendant: 'What happened to you?' 'I was hit playing cricket.' 'Where?' 'At The Oval.' 'Who did it?' 'Thomson.'

The representative of the law then interjected: 'Do you wish to prefer charges?'

Nothing came of that, so cricket awaits its first instance of a writ being served on a fast bowler by a stricken batsman — or his next of kin!

Australian team manager, Fred Bennett, sprang to Thommo's defence that same evening. 'There was nothing wrong with that ball,' he said (the ball that hit Mendis on the head). 'It got up off a length and was a perfectly straight delivery. What do you want him to do, bowl underarm?'

The third match was against West Indies at The Oval, a match played in front of a huge, excited crowd, mainly of West Indian supporters but with a fair smattering of Earls Court Aussies thrown in. All kinds of devices were used for gaining admission. Early in the day a van passed through the Hobbs Gates, ostensibly carrying provisions. Once inside, the rear door was rolled up and out toppled fifteen West Indian fans who bolted for their lives and lost themselves in the already large congregation. Others popped their tickets inside empty beer cans once inside the ground and lobbed them over the old wall to their pals outside. This was the big event of the competition so far, and everyone within range of London wanted to see it.

Australia were always struggling. Put in by Clive Lloyd on a cloudy morning, they lost five wickets for 61 before Ross Edwards and Rod Marsh, with half-centuries apiece, added 99. As Edwards eventually misjudged an off-break from Viv Richards, stepping away to the leg side to hit through cover, Thommo was slumped on a chair in the centre of the dressing-room, sweatered, padded and gloved in readiness, looking so relaxed he might have been planning to turn in.

But it was not his day. He made only a single before holing out off Richards, and then took none for 21 in six overs as the West Indians waltzed home by seven wickets. At least he escaped the kind of mauling Dennis Lillee suffered from the swishing bat of Alvin Kallicharran. Off ten balls from the West Australian, 'Kalli' hit 35 runs, his hooks being especially memorable.

So Australia had to face England in the semi-final, and West Indies were to meet — and overpower — New Zealand.

The semi at Headingley was Gary Gilmour's match. 'Gus' took 6 for 14, making the ball, as Thommo recalls, 'do everything but talk'. England's total of 93 actually seemed enough at one stage, when Australia sank to 39 for the loss of six wickets. But Gilmour came in and, knowing it was his day, thrashed away for 28 not out, clinching the Man of the Match award and a four-wicket win for his side that sent them to Lord's for the first-ever World Cup final.

Jeff Thomson has a few sharp memories of the event:

When we got to Lord's I was still a little bit worried about bowling no-balls. I'd fixed it, but I was a bit nervous about the problem returning. Anyway, I bowled pretty well. I got Greenidge out, but when Clive Lloyd came in I was taken off. I've always bowled pretty well to Lloydy, but he made a hundred that day — he went berserk — and I didn't get called back until much later. I've often thought back on that, and wondered what might've happened if I'd had a longer go at him.

Anyway, they made nearly 300, and the tension was really something as we set about making the runs. We were pacing up and down in the dressing-room, especially towards the later part of the innings, when Dennis and I were soon due out there. We eventually got together for the last wicket with 59 needed, and we really thought the pair of us were going to win the Cup. We were playing the bowling quite easily. It might have been half-past-eight at night, but I was seeing them like a football.

We were hitting the bowling all right, but then Dennis was caught off a no-ball and the crowd — mostly West Indians — thought it was all over and came running onto the field. Meanwhile we'd started running. The bloke who caught it hadn't heard the shout of no-ball, with all the yelling, and he'd thrown the ball across somewhere, while I'm shouting to Dennis, 'Keep running!' and Dennis is hollering the same thing at me.

Then I said, 'Hang on, I don't know who's got the ball! We could be run out.' The ball had gone down towards the Tavern, and that's the last we'd seen of it. We ran a fair few runs, but the umpire was going to give us two!

I said, 'Hey, how much you giving us for that?' And Tom Spencer says 'Two' — real abrupt. 'Pig's arse!' I shouted. 'We've been running up and down here all afternoon. Who are you kidding?' I really got into him. Then I think he changed it.

We'd put on 41 for the last wicket, just 18 short of victory, but when Vanburn Holder came on I couldn't find the ball against the background of the bricks of the pavilion. It was pretty late at night, don't forget. Anyhow, I missed the ball and started to run and Deryck Murray got the ball and underarmed it back and hit the stumps. I was run out. I was exhausted by then, too, from running up and down. It was a flaming long day.

It was a numb feeling, because we weren't all that used to losing. I sat in the dressing-room there and felt really annoyed. I thought, what a bastard; we played wrongly. I think that's why I played a lot better against the West Indians a few months later when they came out to Australia. I really hated losing.

Incredibly, Thommo was the fifth run-out casualty in the Australian innings. Alan Turner and the Chappell brothers were all thrown out by the brilliant Viv Richards, and Max Walker became a fourth victim towards the end, letting Thommo in to join Lillee for their thrilling last-ditch stand.

Everyone was exhausted at the end of that long, long day — players, umpires, scorers, spectators, journalists, possibly even the Duke of Edinburgh, who presented the trophy to West Indies captain, centurymaker and Man of the Match, Clive Lloyd.

Now, though, Ian Chappell's Australians had to pick themselves up for the four-Test series ahead. The international one-day competition, lasting a fortnight, had brought them success that could have been regarded as a bonus. They always felt that limited-overs stuff was far from the real thing, and acknowledged that they had played much less of it than most of their opponents, and were therefore not expected to do all that well.

Nevertheless, it would have been a great turn-up to have won the World Cup, and there was a lingering feeling that they had thrown their chance away with careless running.

With four matches before the first Test, Thommo was still some way short of his peak form. As anticipated, the slow English pitches had drawn a lot of his sting, and the vacillation in his spirits was holding him back.

The match at Southampton gave rise to fresh optimism. He bowled fast, and though he failed to take a wicket, the Hampshire batsmen were seldom at ease. In the second innings the great Barry Richards, on 69, having made a lovely 96 in the first innings, took an agonising blow in the groin and had to retire hurt, and then left-hander David Turner, who had made a century against the previous Australian touring team and 87 in the first innings of this match, had his bottom hand hit, also by Thommo, and retired with a fractured finger. With a not-out 44 in Australia's first innings, Thommo could be said to have been in the picture.

The worry was still there, however, after the match against MCC at Lord's. The only picture he was in now was the hat-trick taken by Bob Woolmer — right in the middle of it, as the Australians lost their last four wickets without a run scored. He took only one wicket, too, in contrast to Dennis Lillee, who fired a noisy salute with ten wickets in the match. Doug Walters made his only century ever at Lord's, and another match was won, Colin Cowdrey bagging a pair after having scored 151 not out a week earlier in Kent's five-wicket victory over the touring team.

Thommo missed that match at Canterbury just as he missed the final run-in game, against Glamorgan, when Greg Chappell blistered to 144 in an hour and a half. All was now ready for the resumption in England-Australia warfare at Edgbaston after a breather of some five months. Were the Australian fast bowlers ready, knives sharpened to make further killings, or would England come back fighting, now that John Snow was back in the side and the effects of the shellshock of the previous series had had time to wear off?

Mike Denness won the toss and defensively put Australia in on an overcast morning, with rain predicted later in the match. He saved his men from an immediate confrontation with their old bogeys, but paid the price in due course — with defeat and loss of the captaincy and his place in the side. Australia made 359 — Marsh 61, McCosker 59, Edwards 56, Ian Chappell 52, Thomson 49 ('I was sure I was going to get my first fifty in Test cricket, but I holed out to mid-off off "Deadly" Underwood. I could have kicked myself. I only needed to pat a single somewhere.').

As soon as Edrich and Amiss began to bat for England, it rained. When play resumed, with the extra hour added, England lost seven wickets for 83 in 2¾ hours.

The tour selectors had stuck with Thommo for the opening Test, despite Gary Gilmour's achievements. But he had little to do with England's collapse. In fact, Chappell took him off after two overs when he sprayed the ball everywhere, clocking up several wides. Max Walker took over and he and Lillee set about demolishing England. They took five wickets each, Lillee for only 15 runs, and England followed on.

This time it was Thommo's turn to take five, and his removal of Amiss, Denness, Gooch (for a 'pair'), Knott and Snow 'gave me a special lot of pleasure after all the muck that had been slung at me'.

England thus went down by an innings, and depression swept the country. Nothing much had changed. The torture was due to continue. It was a thought that cheesed off English cricket-followers the length of the land.

Then came the appointment of the tall, blond, flamboyant, cavalier, aggressive, morale-boosting Tony Greig, as captain — a man who had a date with destiny — or more exactly, with Kerry Packer — in the not-so-distant future. For the moment, it was his angular frame, cap-peak jutting hyper-penetratively, that loped down the steps at

Lord's, giving bright tones of revival to the sight of the England team as it took the field after having scored 315 in the second Test match. And before long, as Australian wickets were snatched at regular intervals, the beery sound of *Rule Britannia* swept across from the Tavern — a sound few had expected to hear this summer.

Thommo, having taken seven wickets in the Derbyshire match and three against Lancashire (as well as swelling his batting average with 48 not out and 4 not out), might well have been close to form once again, but that first day at Lord's found him with severe run-up problems again and trouble with his direction. Twenty-two times he was called for overstepping the crease, and four times he was called for bowling wide. Ian Chappell talked the matter over with rosy-faced Australian-born umpire Bill Alley, but there was no getting away from it: Jeffrey Thomson's stride was wrong and his co-ordination was awry, something like a movie when the sound is a few frames out of 'sync' with the movement.

Lillee did all the early damage, taking 4 for 33 off 10 overs and reducing England to a somewhat familiar 49 for 4 wickets. Then Greig came in to play a valiant innings of 96 and to put on almost 100 with Test debutant David Steele, not quite 34 but grey-haired and bespectacled, and given some tongue from Thommo as well as by most of the other 'Ugly Australians'.

'Who's this? Bloody Father Christmas?' Thommo is alleged to have said in a stage whisper. 'Father Christmas' almost didn't make it to the crease at all, having walked down one staircase too many from the dressing-room and finished in the gents' lavatory in the basement. He eventually emerged up into the sunlight, and made a dramatic and popular half-century before dragging a short one from Thommo into his stumps.

Alan Knott made a very useful 69 before Thommo finished him off too, leg-before. England 315, Australia at one stage seven down for 81. Ross Edwards, who went on to a great 99 before Woolmer got him lbw, then received some precious support from Thommo for the eighth wicket. The fast bowler made only 17, but the stand was worth 52. And then Lillee came in to make not only his highest score in Tests but in all first-class cricket: 73 not out. The last three wickets added 187 runs, and Australia were back in the running.

They were shut out, though, by the tough little left-hander John Edrich, who made 175, and when England declared at 436 for 7, 483 runs ahead, Australia had little choice but to bat it out. Rick McCosker, the Chappells and Ross Edwards saw it safely through, Australia finishing 329 for 3, the real winner being the docile Lord's pitch.

All was not tranquillity between the second and third Tests. Thommo missed the Somerset match but played at Northampton, where a certain Pakistani gentlemen named Sarfraz Nawaz engaged in some pretty basic verbal fisticuffs that came exceedingly close to the real thing. Both like bouncing fast ones at batsmen and both dislike having bouncers bowled at themselves. This led to dissension, and Sarfraz expressed the desire to fight his Australian adversary there and then, having, he said, already reserved a plot in the local cemetery for his body. The slanging match fizzled out, but it made good copy for the 'pop' papers while it lasted, and the vacant grave fortunately was left to await what one can only hope was a much older corpse.

Australia retained the Ashes at Headingley, but in unique circumstances. At 3 for 220, they faced the final day needing a further 225 for victory — a tall task, but who could tell? McCosker was 95 not out, Walters 25. The Chappells may have been out, as was stand-in opener Rod Marsh, but there were still possibilities. But that night the 'Free George Davis' protesters cut up the pitch and poured sump oil on it, and if that wasn't enough, the rain started up around midday. The abandonment left Australia one-up with only the Oval Test to come.

Yet there had been some exceptional performances in this Leeds Test. David Steele, old Father Christmas himself, had added to his 50 and 45 at Lord's further, bigger innings of 73 and 92, often playing bravely forward to the fast bowlers when others would have played half-cock if not right back. How would he have gone in Australia, when all the shrapnel was flying in '74-75? people were asking. Would have got his bloody head knocked off, thought Thommo and many others.

Gary Gilmour had come in for Alan Turner in this Test, and took nine wickets in the match, ramming home the suspicion that he should have played in all the Tests. England's main gain was Phil Edmonds, the slow left-arm bowler, who picked up five rather jittery Australian wickets for 28 at his first attempt in Test cricket. Thommo, on his twenty-fifth birthday, was caught by Steele off John Snow for 16 made in an hour.

So with the shock of the Headingley vandalism still evident throughout the game in England, the final Test came, with Thommo in particular glad that the flight back home was only a few days away.

But there were a few more hardships yet to endure. Australia piled up over 500 runs in the Oval Test (Greg Chappell and Jeff Thomson — magnificently caught at slip first ball by Chris Old — making Queensland's contribution to that total precisely nil!) and then rolled England over for 191 (Thommo getting Woolmer and three tailenders for 50). Ian Chappell, having made 192 in his last match as captain and seen his side do the sort of thing it had been doing most of last Australian season, did what he had to do by making England follow on. This time they dropped anchor, Bob Woolmer making the slowest-ever century in England-Australia Tests, Edrich 96, Roope 77, Steele (getting closer and closer to Christmas) 66, Knott 64, Barry Wood 22 in almost three hours.

The Australians were in the field from late on Friday until tea on

Wednesday, and not one of them was not footsore by the end of it. Thommo's memories are bitter, though he recognises that it was the supreme battle:

In the last Test we made a mistake: we made too many runs! Over five hundred. We rolled England for about 190 and sent them back in, then it was the big drag. They blocked the guts out of us. Up and down those stairs at The Oval, day after day. I'm not kidding, it was like a torture. Up and down the stairs, out and bowl, up and down the stairs. It was unbelievable. We bowled a million overs each, Dennis, myself, Max and Rowdy. Even the Chappells bowled, and 'Freddie' Walters. I believe even Ross Edwards had a couple of overs — and got carted. Woolmer made the slowest-ever hundred in England-Australia Tests. I was sick of the sight of his arse.

But at least it was real Test cricket. You can't tell me that what they were playing in 1978-79 was real Test cricket. It was a farce. Just second-rate. That's where it's diabolical. What should have happened is that there should have been a mixture of the World Series Australians and the side that played as the Test team. Only a couple of the Test players would have made the grade. It would have packed every ground out, and that's the way it should've been. That's what the crowds want. It's also what the cricketers want. The only people who didn't seem to want it were the Australian Cricket Board.

They reckon it's a democracy!

To return to the final Test of '75, the air in the dressing-room was not so much heavy with the sweet smell of tired feet as with blue oaths — aimed at the English batsmen, the groundsman, Pressmen, anything at all that made the suffering bowlers and fieldsmen feel better.

Before the match had ground as far as the agonising last couple of days, I had been up to see Dennis Lillee and Jeff Thomson to persuade them to attend the launching of a book I had written called *The Fast Men*. They had time to look through an advance copy, and Lillee carefully perused the references to him in the book — and passed them for accuracy — apart from the statement that he had once bowled a beamer at Bob Willis. 'The ball slipped!' he claimed indignantly.

Thommo mainly studied the pictures. And I plainly recall his amazement at one. 'Hey, look at this guy, Dennis. He must've been *real* fast. He's bowlin' with his bloody hat on!'

It was Learie Constantine. And there was no doubting how fast and unpleasant his bowling could be. Perhaps he managed to keep his cap on because he didn't have magnificent collar-length hair to defy its wearing.

Anyway, how often has Thommo been seen in a cap? His Australian Test headgear is a prime exhibit in my private cricket museum. The original owner needed it even less than his great forebear Keith Miller needed a cap.

The 1975 tour gave England a chance to see the mighty Thommo, but it rarely saw him at his best. For a spell here and a spell there he approached the crease with rhythm and bounce, and sent the ball screaming down to the far end and beyond. But there was something missing — usually in the pitch itself. He harboured thoughts that he and Lillee were being got at, perhaps not realising that pitches in England had been sluggish for years, and young quick bowlers in that country soon learnt that to strive for sheer speed was to risk a quick exit from the professional game, spirit broken. The thing to do, as any county coach would be swift to point out, was cut the pace and concentrate on accuracy: line and length, the ancient English cricket angelus.

He'd taken 16 wickets in the four Tests at 28.56 apiece — a rather different set of figures from those of the '74-75 rubber. Still, he had taken 49 English Test wickets in under a year, and that was something special.

He'd also been featured (with Dennis Lillee) in a Trog cartoon on the front cover of *Punch*; he'd dealt patiently with hosts of admirers after play — sometimes risking an appearance in the Lord's Tavern when barely a sentence could be completed without interruption from somebody wanting a slip of paper autographed or wishing to buy him a beer; and he'd been compared, tongue-in-cheek, by Ian Wooldridge of the *Daily Mail* with Titian's painting of the god Bacchus, now in the National Gallery. The comparison so delighted the Gallery that the item was put on show in the Exhibition.

He'd been featured in *Radio Times,* smiling toothfully and lending his name to a true-to-character quote: 'Once I'm out on that pitch I just have to find out what the batsman doesn't like and then land it on him . . . As long as I can get plenty of sleep, I reckon I can cope with anything.' He'd also been featured, with John Snow, surrounded by delectable ladies from several countries, in a woman's magazine fashion spread. All very image-building.

His image was further enhanced when artist Rosemary Taylor used a dramatic side view of Thommo for one of her impressionistic canvases and a rear view for another.

But the adaptation of his supposed personality which most captured the public imagination was — to return to the *Daily Mail's* outstanding sportswriter — that of Ian Wooldridge, who created 'Terror Tomkins', ace Aussie fast bowler, king of malapropism, Pom-hater-in-chief — to judge from his cartoon portrait a cross between Lillee and Thomson but, to judge from much of the text of his fictional 'letters to Mum', so clearly Thommo in caricature.

'At London Airport,' Tomkins told his Mum early in the tour, 'they waved all the abbos straight through immigration and made us get on the end of a queue about ten miles long. "Come on, let's pizzoff," said my oppo, Dennis, but I said "No, let's stay and kill an extra couple of their batsmen." It just shows how the Establishment works in England, because by the time we got to Lord's they'd changed all the laws of cricket so that you couldn't bowl bouncers in the World Cup.'

It was one of the best reads of the summer. And Wooldridge's editor must have thought so too, for 'Terror' lived on through another tour and into 1979. In four years he'd become a little more serious, as these samples show:

1975: 'They also tried to con us into playing two warm-up matches against some place called Gloucestershire. Well, we jumped at that because we thought that was right next door to Chelsea, where all the birds are. Not at all. We were thinking about Gloucester-*road*. Gloucester*shire* is bloody nearly in Chicago. It's wild west country so we told them to stuff it and sorted out the local talent. You can't move for birds here. They've got this thing called the Permissible Society.'

1979: 'Even the Customs bloke was sivil. "Yore Terror Tomkins the famous Orstralian thunderbolt bowler what nearly delapitated some of our best batsmen and now rites occasional belles lettres wot nobody can understand for the *Daily Mail* ain't yer?" he inquired. "Wossit got ter do with you yer interfering Pommie bastard?" I smiled. "That's my Terror," he contorted. "Always the one with the ready repast. Now, have yer got rabies or kolera or been in contact with that Kerry Packer?" '

CHAPTER 6

World Champs

The 1975-76 series between Australia and West Indies was regarded as the world championship of Test cricket. Few could have foreseen how the tourists would crumble before the Australian fast attack and the superb batsmanship of new captain Greg Chappell, supported by old hand, Ian Redpath (three centuries), Ian Chappell, new men Gary Cosier and Graham Yallop, all-rounder Gary Gilmour, Turner, Marsh and McCosker. Australia won five of the Tests and somehow went to pieces momentarily in the second, at Perth, where West Indies won by an innings.

Thommo was wicket-taker-in-chief, with 29 at 28.65, two more than Lillee but slightly costlier. This time the main support came from Gilmour, who topped the bowling averages with 20 wickets at 20.30 — and also thrashed a valuable 95 at Adelaide.

So the Australian public, for the second summer running, had almost an uninterrupted feast of victory, much to its liking. And its cricketers, if idols already, moved into the super-idol class. At the same time, of course, as history now knows, they moved ever nearer a revolution that was to bring them rewards more in keeping with entertainers who kept the populace glued to radio and television, their minds diverted from economic anxieties.

It is not as if the West Indians were a second-rate bunch. Viv Richards was as yet an unknown quantity, but Andy Roberts was close to being the world's fastest bowler, and took as many as 22 wickets in this series, and Michael Holding showed much promise. Keith Boyce had rattled England two years previously, and in some quarters Bernard Julien was thought of very highly. Vanburn Holder brought experience to the ranks, and the veteran off-spinner Lance Gibbs had lost little of his cunning. The batting line-up was potentially devastating: Clive Lloyd, Gordon Greenidge, Roy Fredericks, Alvin Kallicharran, Lawrence Rowe (a Test triple-centurymaker), and Richards. No worries in the wicketkeeping department either, with the world's most experienced Test 'keeper in Deryck Murray.

It says much for the Australians that they overthrew all that talent by the resounding margin of five Tests to one.

How was it done? The simple truth was that the home side played to their limits and often beyond, while West Indian morale and temperament let them down. It was acknowledged that the party was short on discipline, and when things started to go wrong on the field there was a certain disintegration that had been known with previous West Indian sides — and which Tony Greig tried so catastrophically to define a few months later when he said they 'grovel' when they're down. He and his men paid dearly for this in the Test matches of 1976.

In 1975-76 it was Clive Lloyd's men who paid. At Brisbane, where Greg Chappell made two centuries in his debut Test as captain, they went down by eight wickets, despite a second-innings recovery in which Rowe and Kallicharran made centuries. Then came the amazing comeback at Perth, where Ian Chappell made 156 only for West Indies to pile up 585 runs, Fredericks hitting a dazzling 169 and Lloyd 149. Roberts then gave a perfect exhibition of the fast bowler's craft in taking 7 for 54, and Australia wondered what the season held in store.

The third Test, beginning on Boxing Day at Melbourne, put Australia back in command, and it was not without significance that for the first time in the series Thommo was on song. With only one wicket (his 50th in Tests) in the first match and three in the second, it was time for him to have better luck. He had been bowling explosively throughout the season, having a few 'highs', such as his first-ever ten-in-a-match when he took 6 for 47 and 4 for 73 for Queensland against Western Australia at Perth, and the occasional 'low', as when Roy Fredericks caned him in the Perth Test (Thommo came off with figures for his opening spell of 3-0-33-0). Now, with Greg Chappell putting West Indies in on a wicket with a touch of green about it, Thommo, narrowly winning the vote over Gilmour for inclusion showed the crowd of almost 86,000 that he — not his mate Lillee, nor this guy Roberts, or the newcomer Holding — was the fastest bowler on Earth.

After 35 minutes Greenidge was the first to 'cop it' — caught behind by Marsh from an outswinger. Then three balls later the sharp click of another roaring delivery as it made fleeting contact with Rowe's bat-edge sent a catch to Ian Chappell at slip — his hundredth in Tests.

Thommo's next success came with his return after lunch this hot day. Kallicharran fanned at a rearing ball and was taken at the wicket. And soon he had his fourth wicket, earned by a skilful change of pace as Fredericks, 59, put a catch up to mid-off.

The fifth wicket came — yet again to Thommo — when Lloyd played back and edged to Greg Chappell, and West Indies were five down for 108. Lillee did the rest, and Thommo finished with 5 for 62 in 11 overs, his first return of five wickets in a Test for ten innings. It may have cost him a strained abdominal muscle, but it was comforting to be among the wickets again, and to end that nonsense talk about him becoming twelfth man.

Australia, thanks to a five-hour century from Redpath and a century in his first Test innings by Cosier, went well ahead, making 485 to lead by 261, and on the third evening West Indies lost three for 92, with

Thommo, having hit 44 off 47 balls, feeling too uncomfortable to bowl. But he had a round of golf on the rest day and some treatment from a physiotherapist, and pronounced himself to his captain as 'happy' and expecting to be able to bowl flat out the next day. It was important that he should do so, for the Sydney Test match followed this one straightaway, and the selectors would be treating his performance as a fitness trial.

He began well, beating Viv Richards for pace and having him caught behind, and at lunch he had one for 23 off five overs, with West Indies tottering at 5 for 175. But afterwards Clive Lloyd gave one of his special displays, sharing 17 runs with Murray off a Thomson over and hitting four fours off a Mallett over. The West Indies skipper got his hundred, but Australia needed only 52 to win, and got them for the loss of two wickets, taking a two-one lead in the series.

The pattern persisted in the next Test, which, like the previous three, was finished on the fourth day. This time, back in his native town, Thommo turned it on for his family and pals with nine wickets in a Test for the second time — and a duck in his only innings.

His big effort was needed perhaps as never before or since, because for the first time in his Test career he was missing his 'other half', Dennis Lillee, who was declared unfit with a chest infection. Greg Chappell won the toss and yet again put West Indies in.

Thommo was erratic — which is not always much help to the batsmen. But in his third over he broke makeshift opener Julien's thumb, and when he swung round to the Randwick end he had Kallicharran caught by Redpath wide at slip. That was Australia's only success before lunch, but during an action-packed afternoon he had Fredericks spectacularly caught high at slip by Ian Chappell after having Rowe missed by Cosier at slip, and when the tigerish Lloyd came in he sent a ball flying up off a length to smack his jaw and send him off for repairs.

After tea there was more for the crowd of over 50,000 to scream about. Deryck Murray hooked Thommo for a brilliant six, but several overs later, when the same batsman carted Walker high over square leg, Thommo made the catch of a lifetime, running fast for 35 yards, diving at the ball, holding it, and sliding along the turf — this despite having bowled 18 overs. That made it 4 for 213, but by the close West Indies had forged ahead to 286 for the loss of six.

Eventually they reached a respectable 355, Thomson's third wicket coming when a hesitant Michael Holding hit his wicket as he played back. And after tea on the second day Australia found themselves four down for 103. It might have been worse, for Ian Chappell seemed to be caught behind off Holding but received the benefit of the umpire's decision. Holding broke down in tears of frustration, Kallicharran spent some time gesticulating, and the West Indians lost their poise.

Worse followed for them, when one of the most fateful dropped catches in Test history occurred. Greg Chappell, on 11, was missed by Boyce at slip off Roberts, and went on to a glorious 182 not out, carrying his team to 405, a lead of 50. There was no looking back.

On the third evening West Indies lost three early wickets through irresponsible batting, all hooking, Kallicharran off Thommo's bowling and Richards to a wonderful diving catch by him at square leg. Next day the collapse continued — 128 all out, Jeff Thomson 6 for 50, twice having shot a stump clean out of its hole.

The victory was by seven wickets, and Thommo, having taken the Man of the Match award in the previous Test (plus a magnum of champagne for each of his two sixes), was content to make way for his captain this time. Greg Chappell, whom Thommo regarded with the utmost respect, now averaged 132 as captain of Australia and was obviously thriving on his work.

The Adelaide Test saw Australia forge further ahead: four-one with one to play. This fifth contest was memorable for centuries by Redpath, Turner and Viv Richards (beginning his gigantic scoring run in Tests throughout 1976), and scores of 95 by Gilmour and Boyce. But most of all it signalled Lance Gibbs' equalling Fred Trueman's record of 307 wickets, a figure he was to pass in the final Test.

Thommo took six more wickets in Australia's 190-run win, for once avoiding his Adelaide injury jinx, and picked up four more in the last innings of the series, at Melbourne, where he polished the match off by having Lance Gibbs caught by Marsh. He had the chance to finish the match earlier, when West Indies, nine down in the first innings, needed one run to avoid the follow-on. Thommo saved them with a no-ball to Holder. His comment isn't recorded, though, as Ian Chappell said, he can be harder on himself verbally than on any opponent.

So they had done it — beaten the talented but temperamentally suspect West Indians comprehensively. And they were entitled to call themselves world champions. Thommo had regained his reputation, after early doubts, that he was probably the fieriest bowler in the world — and one of the wildest: he sent down no fewer than 58 no-balls and 15 wides during the six Tests. But it was his 29 wickets that mattered — plus the odd flash of Olympian fielding and catching.

The usually sparkling West Indians had been reduced to prolonged bouts of bitter misery, and the notably courteous and placid Clive Lloyd had several times uttered condemnation of the umpiring. But he also wrote of his respect for Jeff Thomson: 'He is a deceptive bowler, so very strong, and once he settles on a good line he keeps going. I took a few runs off him in the World Cup final at Lord's but even so I developed a respect for him there and then.'

Thommo was obviously thinking harder about his game now. His image may not have changed, but many keen judges felt that he had matured beyond expectation in the year since he had been let loose on the Englishmen.

Certainly his bowling method, as spelt out in the following paragraphs, is as instinctive and unhelpful to opposing batsmen as was Maurice Tate's in the old days:

I might as well say a few words here about my method of bowling. I used to favour the inswinger because the inswinging bouncer to a right-hander has him in a lot of trouble, especially if it pitches wide of off stump and comes in at him, and he tries to duck. That's how I used to hit a lot of blokes. Then I started to develop the outswinger, and used it with the occasional bit of in-dip. Keeps 'em guessing. I do it all just with a bit of wrist, and the batsman can't pick that up.

With my side-on action I can't really bowl chest-on, so I have to vary my delivery just through wrist action. Maybe I'll bowl closer to the stumps, but I don't make it obvious. I can sit and watch blokes on the TV now and you can tell what they're going to bowl as they come in. You can see it a mile off. But they still might get a wicket with it.

When I'm coaching I tell fellas to use the width of the crease, but I don't really bother with that myself. I'm lucky. I can do it all with a flick of the wrist.

I can just recall a game when everything went well, and I ended up with my best figures in first-class cricket — 7 for 33 and twelve wickets in the match, against New South Wales in Brisbane in 1976-77. We got them out for 71 and made them follow on. I got five more wickets in the second dig, but 'Gus' Gilmour came in and thrashed a century. I believe he said something to the newspaper blokes about enjoying batting against me. Not too many blokes have said that, I can tell you! I was getting a bit tired when he came in, but I'm not taking anything away from him. He's a very handy player and he played very well to get that hundred.

He played in all eight Sheffield Shield matches for Queensland that season of 1975-76 and helped them to their third successive year as runners-up. Their luck was cruel. They lost only at Adelaide, and won four matches before rain — gallons and gallons of it — ruined their last three games. In all, 51 hours' play was lost to Queensland through bad weather, and they were doomed to wait a few years more for their first Sheffield Shield.

There were some amusing and some grim moments during the domestic season. In the opening match, against his old State, Thommo was dismissed by his old pal Lenny Pascoe in both innings, the second time without scoring. In Perth he bagged ten wickets in the match to send Western Australia, the champions, reeling, but a back strain restricted him in the second innings against South Australia (the Adelaide jinx again). He was back with a vengeance at Sydney, taking seven wickets (including Pascoe!) and breaking Len Richardson's arm with a vicious kicker. It was not as if the batsman had just come to the crease. He was on 87 at the time, and the incident was yet a further reminder of how Thommo could surprise even an established batsman with his steep lift.

That was it, then, for another season. He had put a lot in and got a lot out. Now it was time for an easing-off, with another busy season to follow, and beyond that, a second trip to England.

1 It is hard to associate the young Thommo (back row, second left) in this Punchbowl
High School third grade team with the scourge of the world's batsmen he was to become
only a few years later

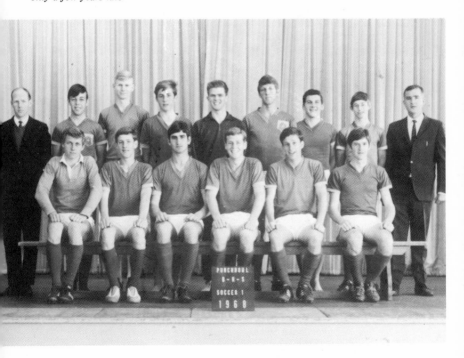

2 Thommo went to Punchbowl High School with Len Pascoe, playing soccer as well as
cricket. They appear in this picture unaware that almost ten years later they would be
Australia's opening bowlers in the Jubilee Test match at Lord's

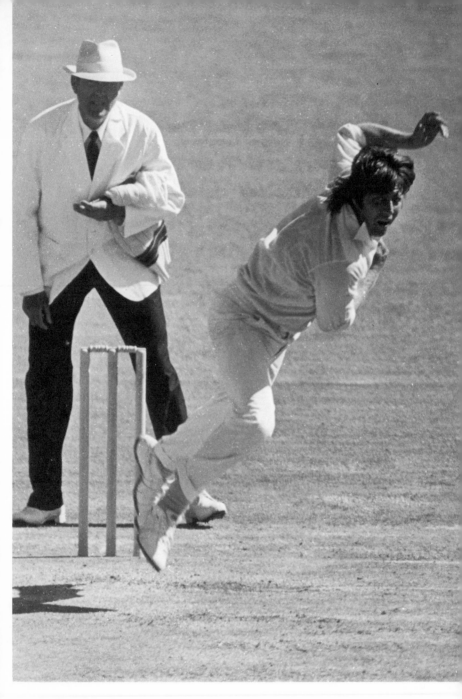

3 By the time this photograph was taken during the second Test at Perth, the 1974-75 visiting English cricketers knew that they were up against a new fast bowling phenomenon. Thommo had already taken 9 of their wickets in the first Test at Brisbane, was to leave Perth with a further 7, and finish his part in the series with 33 — he missed the last Test through injury

4 & 5 *When 42-year-old veteran Colin Cowdrey was called from the depth of an English winter to reinforce the tottering English side during the 1974-75 series, Thommo's reaction was 'He'll cop it as quick as anyone!' Bravely though Cowdrey played, Thommo's pace was altogether too much for him, and here he bowls him at Perth and traps him leg-before at Melbourne*

6 & 7 *After his major role in Australia's regaining of the Ashes in the 1974-75 series, Thommo went to England for the 1975 World Cup tournament. English cricket fans saw him 'live' for the first time (above) and were mightily impressed at his speed even on the slow English wickets. Australia had a tough tussle with Pakistan (below) in their opening match of the tournament, eventually losing out to the West Indies in a final made memorable by the clash between Thommo, Dennis Lillee and the magnificent West Indies batsmen*

8 & 9 After the World Cup tournament Australia played England in a 4-match Test series. In the first Test England's captain Mike Denness (above), who had already suffered nightmarishly at Thommo's hands during the 1974-75 series in Australia, once again found his speed too hard to handle and he was quite literally bowled out of the England captaincy and Test cricket. In the same match Thommo and fellow pace assassin Dennis Lillee each took 5 wickets in an innings, and for good measure Thommo scored 49 runs in Australia's only innings. Here he leaves the field with Dennis Lillee at the end of that knock

10 Thommo finds himself on the receiving end of a bouncer from England's Peter Lever at Lord's in 1975. Little quarter was given to fellow fast bowlers during the war of the bouncer in the Ashes series of the 1970s

11 Thommo watches Ian Chappell catch Lawrence Rowe off his bowling during the third Test against the West Indies at Melbourne, 1975. It was Chappell's 100th Test catch. Also watching intently are Rod Marsh and Greg Chappell whose behind-the-stumps and slip catching off Thommo's bowling has been outstanding

12 *Thommo's no slouch in the field. Here he dives to take a brilliant catch in the out-field off Max Walker's bowling and dismiss West Indies batsman Deryck Murray during the fourth Test at Sydney, 1976*

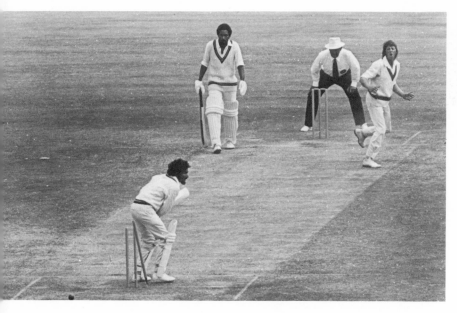

13 *In the same match he again dismissed Deryck Murray, but this time in the way he loves best — removing a stump from the ground and sending it cartwheeling back to the wicketkeeper*

14 Considering the shocking shoulder damage he sustained during the Test series against Pakistan 1976-77, and the loss to World Series Cricket of his joint-spearhead Dennis Lillee, Thommo bowled magnificently in the 1977 Ashes series played in England. He captured 23 wickets, England captain Mike Brearley being a victim in this second Test at Old Trafford, caught by Greg Chappell, centre

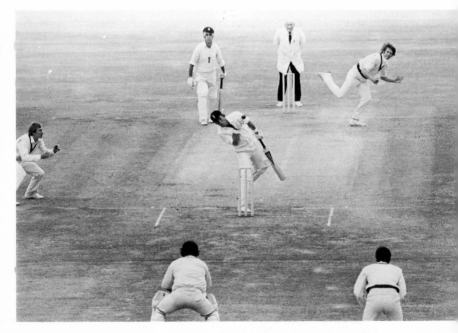

15 Despite his undoubted courage England batsman Dennis Amiss never came to terms with the pace of Thommo or Dennis Lillee. By the time this photograph of him weaving away from yet another of Thommo's fast deliveries was taken at Old Trafford, his Test career against Australia was nearing its end

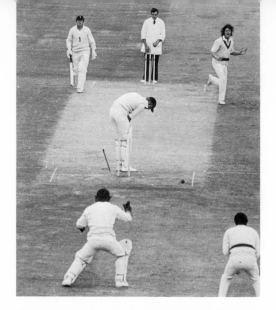

16 That ever-combative cricketer Tony Greig has always been a prize wicket for Australian bowlers to capture, and here Thommo removes his middle stump during the third Test at Trent Bridge

17 Thommo in full cry during the Trent Bridge Test. Non-striker Geoff Boycott is on the way to his return-to-Test-cricket century, but Thommo eventually dismissed him to end the 7-hour marathon innings

18 Thommo with Bob Simpson durir
the 1977-78 Test series against Indi
Simpson had been recalled to lead Au
tralia after a ten-year retirement, ar
to Thommo's great delight he w
appointed vice-captain for the tour
West Indies that followed this series

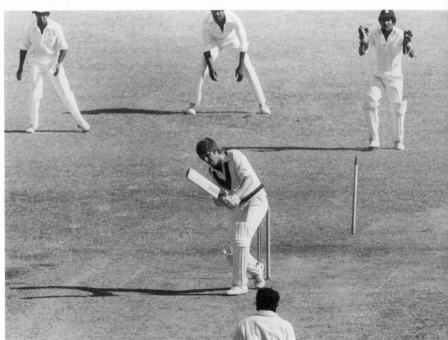

19 There are no half measures about Thommo's batting. He likes to make runs in a
hurry or perish in the attempt — as he does here convincingly to West Indies paceman
Joel Garner during the second Test at Barbados, 1978. Wicketkeeper Deryck Murray
would have appreciated this sight (see photograph 13)

20 & 21 West Indies opening batsman Gordon Greenidge reels after being hit by a ball from Thommo during the Barbados Test. Thommo dismissed Greenidge for 8 in the first innings but honours were even after Greenidge put together a fine 80 not out in the second. In the same match Thommo's tremendous bowling performance in the West Indies first innings brought him figures of 6 for 77, and he fully deserved the applause of his team-mates as they left the field at the end of that innings

22 & 23 *An agreement between the Australian Cricket Board and World Series Cricket allowed Thommo to take part in WSC's tour of West Indies early in 1979, and to team up again with Dennis Lillee, the Chappells, Rod Marsh and Max Walker. Here he is bowling in the third Supertest at Trinidad (below to Clive Lloyd) where he took 5 for 78 in the West Indies first innings.*

24 Patrick Eagar's superb photograph and David Frith's graphic description capture
the split second before Thommo releases the ball. '... the final supercharged sweep of
the arm. The mouth stretches grotesquely; the eyes protrude; the hair stands up like a
cock's comb'

25 & 26 Memorable milestones: Thommo is congratulated by his colleagues (above) after taking his first Test wicket at Brisbane against England, November 1974. Only 22 Tests later, at The Oval, August 1977, he secured his 100th Test wicket (below), once more his victim being an English batsman Graham Roope. By the end of that Test, his 14th against England, he had taken 72 of the old enemy's wickets

27 *Thommo looks on as Australian women cricket's 'Thommo', Raelee Thompson, who opens the bowling for their Test team, shows classic pace bowling style during a match played in Queensland to promote women's cricket. The likeness of the followthrough in the bowling actions of the two 'Thommos' is remarkable. (See photograph 17)*

28 *Thommo and his close friend Len Pascoe toured England with the 1977 Australian team. Here they take a break from watching the action during a county match with a spot of dressing-room soccer — possibly reliving the days when they played in the same school soccer side*

29 & 30 Swimming — even if it's not exactly the Pacific surf — and golf provide Thom-mo with relaxing moments during strenuous overseas tours with Australian cricket teams. This golf swing might have been effective had Thommo used it in photograph 19!

CHAPTER 7

Catastrophe at Adelaide

There was no reason why the 1976-77 season should not have been even better than those preceding it, except that a savage injury was lurking ahead of him — a setback so serious that it seemed certain his playing days were over.

It was the season of Queensland's cricket centenary, and at a special race meeting in Brisbane in September one of the events was named in his honour: the Jeff Thomson Flying Handicap. It served as a reminder of that old-time super-athlete, C.B. Fry, who, having conquered every field of human activity he had entered, announced he was taking an interest in horse-racing and would be making his debut in a few weeks' time. 'What as,' enquired a friend, 'owner, jockey or horse?'

Thommo didn't compete against the geegees, but he did create a fair amount of confusion in grade cricket circles when he went to net practice with Easts, who happily chose him for the opening match. He then upped and went back to Toombul, with whom he continued playing. This was small consolation for Dave Cunningham, who, anticipating no place for himself in an Easts attack consisting of Thommo and former Test fastie Tony Dell, had moved to Wynnum-Manly.

The improved pitches at Brisbane's Gabba ground, now cared for by John Maley, who was to make such a reputation for himself in preparing the World Series 'greenhouse' pitches, were an incentive to all the Queensland players, and Thommo forgot any plans to move back to Sydney now. Here he was, playing in a special one-day celebration match for the QCA Centenary, and bowling to Geoff Boycott for the first time.

The controversial Yorkshire run-accumulator had withdrawn his services from England's Test team just before the 1974-75 tour of Australia, having allowed his name to be included in the originally-chosen side. Now, after two years of international exile, he flew from Sydney, where he was playing grade cricket for Waverley, to appear in the all-star Invitation XI.

Queensland batted first and made 283 for 7 in 40 overs, Viv Richards, straight off the aircraft from the Caribbean, thrashing a century which cost him two bats. The Invitation XI got off to a terrible start, losing three for 15, but recovered to make 216 thanks to 89 from Doug Walters.

The Boycott-Thomson duel was soon over. Thommo sent down a trimmer that touched the inside of Boycott's bat as it homed in on the middle stump. The Englishman had made only four. Ian Chappell was no luckier. Thommo produced a beautiful yorker for him and shattered his stumps when he was 22.

Thommo was writing — or offering thoughts to a ghost-writer — for a newspaper now, and for the first time he said something about his preference of ends: 'Many people have claimed I'm a better bowler in the second spell, or with an older ball. That's a load of garbage even though success seems to come that way more often than not. I feel just as much at home with any condition of the ball.'

While ruing the fact that he was nursing an arm injury 'that isn't serious' he paid tribute to his skippers: 'I'm lucky to have had the Chappells in charge with their shrewd bowling changes and top-rate field placings. If I don't get any wickets, that's my fault — not the skipper's. Dennis has more to say about his field placings, but then that's his bag. He likes being involved in that way. To me, it's the skipper's job.'

In the opening Shield match he and his skipper did a good job on the Victorians at Brisbane. He took seven wickets in the match, which was won by an innings, and prompted Greg Chappell to say that he was bowling as fast as ever. In the light drizzle and fading light no man on Earth would have fancied facing him.

He took only one wicket in the drawn Western Australia match, but a 5 for 32 helped bundle South Australia out for a second time for just under 100 and took Queensland to another innings victory, and once more Shield hopes were rising.

The fourth match, still at home, brought Thommo his best match return in first-class cricket to the time of writing: 12 for 112. The sufferers were New South Wales, and his seven first-innings victims were Davis, Turner, McCosker, Walters, Toohey, Rixon and Pascoe, McCosker being his 200th wicket. At one stage they were 8 for 47, but they eventually managed 71, their lowest ever against Queensland. When Thommo's old State followed on he took two more wickets that evening — nine in the day's play.

Gilmour made his superb century next day, but Queensland went on to a five-wicket win and were hot favourites for the Shield. Once again, though, anticlimax was to follow, caused in part by the absence of key players in New Zealand or, in Thommo's case, by injury.

All was well up to the first Test against Pakistan. In fact life could not have seemed rosier. Jeffrey Thomson had married Cheryl Wilson, with Greg Chappell as best man, the bride 'absolutely stunning' in her white chiffon and lace gown and the bridegroom in velvet. As the best man kissed the bride, Thommo observed: 'Me skipper's outdone me already.' Then he embraced Cheryl and said, 'Now I might get a bowl.'

What were his first words to her as they stood together as man and wife? 'Cripes, mate, you've got me there,' he murmured.

Australia's fastest bowler and highest-paid sportsman had stated his attitude clearly enough before the wedding: 'You get jack of running around all the time, especially when there is something loving and caring for you waiting at home. Seriously, I'm a one-girl man.'

That girl was soon to find herself unexpectedly sitting anxiously beside her man as he lay in a hospital bed in Adelaide.

He'd taken two wickets on the opening day of that opening Test match against Pakistan when, bowling to Zaheer after lunch, he forced the batsman into an indecisive pull. The pull spooned up and Thommo dashed in for the catch. Unfortunately, so too did Alan Turner, and there was the most almighty crash as they collided. Umpire Max O'Connell said later that he heard Thomson's shoulder crack like a pistol shot. Both players lay motionless for some time as their teammates signalled frantically for medical assistance. Thommo remembers the disaster and its aftermath:

It was easily the worst injury I've suffered, that one at Adelaide at Christmas 1976. I bowled a bouncer at Zaheer Abbas, and there was no way he could've hooked it. He just popped it up. It lobbed next to the pitch. I looked around, and nobody was near the catch. Alan Turner was at midwicket, so I thought, Geez, I'd better go for this. I ran for it, and dived full-length, and just as I was diving I just saw out the corner of my eye, just six foot away, a bloke also coming for the catch. Next second, Crash! He landed straight down on top of my right arm while I was still in the air.

I didn't feel a lot of pain — until I tried to use the arm to get up! I thought, Shit, my arm won't move, you know? I remember getting up, and seeing Turner still down there, dead as a maggot. I felt like laying the boot into him! I got up and I was cursing. If I could have bowled then I would have bowled the quickest in my life!

I said to the other blokes, 'Hang on a minute; I'll see if I can get my arm over.' But the arm was just torn away. If the collarbone had broken it would have been fairly easy, but the ligaments were all torn away, and the shoulder was hanging.

We went up into the dressing-room, I remember, and the bloke had to cut my shirt off. (I still use that shirt. It was a good one. I got it stitched up again, and I bowl in it. I wouldn't give it away for quids. I'm funny like that. Accidents don't worry me, I'm not superstitious. You can see the sewing mark across from the buttons to the shoulder. The scar on my shoulder is another mark to remind me.)

I said to the physio, 'What can you do with this; I've got to get out there and bowl?' He looked at it and said, 'We'd better get a doctor!' Being quite pig-headed, I said, 'Don't get a doctor; just get a bloke to put this back in and I'll get on back out there.'

He was a quiet bloke, and I'm sometimes a rowdy bloke, so it was quite a scene. Then this little bloke comes in and says in a soft voice, 'Can I have a look?'

'What d'you reckon?' I said. And he said he'd probably have to operate on it and put a pin in and all that. I said, 'Pig's arse! And anyway, mate,' I said, 'who are you? What would you know about it? I'm waiting for the doctor to come in.'

You guessed it: he was the doctor. And he was the one who eventually did the job on the shoulder. We went to the hospital, and had to wait about an hour. My wife, Cheryl, waited with me. I remember going into the operating theatre, and the blokes round the table were joking and carrying on. I said a few things to them, and my last words were, 'Listen, you'd better fix this thing up properly because I'm going back to the motel tomorrow. I want to be out of here tomorrow, so get that for a start! It's Christmas Day tomorrow and the boys are having a party, and I want to be there, right? Fix this thing up and I'm leaving in the morning, okay?'

Anyhow, the surgeon says, 'Well, we'll just see how you feel when you wake up.' I'd never been operated on before.

I woke up in the recovery room. It was a funny feeling. There I was, battling like hell to open my eyes. The eyelids were so heavy. I could hear noises, and there was a nurse, waiting, checking on me and all that sort of thing. She said, 'You woke up quick.' I said, 'Yeah, I want to get out of here. When are they going to take me in and do me?'

She said, 'You're done. Have a look!'

I could see this huge bandage on my arm. She must've been right. You know how your speech is slurred when you get out of the anaesthetic? Well, I'm trying to talk away there, saying 'I'm right now. Get me out of here. Back to me room at the motel.'

The nurse said, 'You just wait there. I'll be in charge here. You might be in charge out there on the cricket field, but I'm in charge here.'

Back in the ward I was half-asleep, but the aching in my shoulder, from my head right down my neck and all round the shoulder, where all the muscles were torn — Geez, the pain! I was on morphine, a shot every couple of hours. I had pillows stacked behind me, sitting there like a mummy. Whenever they came in to give me another needle, I'd say, 'Look, I'm leaving here in the morning. I want to get out.'

Come six o'clock in the morning, I'd had no real sleep because it was aching too much, and I thought, the only way I'm going to get out of this joint is to pretend I'm right. So I got out of bed while nobody was around, and my first steps, I'm not kidding, I went arse over head, I was that rubber-legged. The bloody sling around my neck was wearing into the flesh, and my injured arm felt terrifically heavy.

I'm walking round the ward, trying to look as if I'm okay, and by about eight o'clock the doctor had come, and the nurse said, 'If the doctor says you can go after you've walked around the room, that's all right.'

I walked round that room, but Geez, it nearly killed me. I could hardly move. But he said it was all right for me to go. So I got a cab and went back to the motel for Christmas morning. It was the worst thing I ever did. I no sooner got into the motel than the wound was aching, which meant a doctor had to come out all the time. Sometimes he'd be late because he was called away somewhere else, and when the morphine wore off before he got there — Ugh! I tell you . . .

The players had a Christmas dinner, but as it turned out, I couldn't go along. They ended up coming round to see me, I think. I can't really remember, that's how out to it I was, on drugs, high!

When the painkiller wore off, I was smashing bottles and glasses. The pain was just so much. I nearly flaked. Once, when the doctor was an hour late, I started hurling glasses against the wall. It was killing me. Poor Cheryl just sat there through it. I couldn't do anything about it. Nor could she.

I was under treatment for several days, and finally they said I'd be all right to travel, so I came home in the plane. Back in Brisbane I put a bed in the TV room so I could watch the cricket, swallowing painkillers. A few more days and it wore off, once you got used to not depending on the morphine.

Immediately I started exercising. I used an enlarged squash ball, just squeezing it, and Tom Dooley gave me a course of exercises. Apart from Adrian Munyard, who did the operation in Adelaide, and Donald Beard, the doctor who organised it all, being busy himself at the time, I owe most to Tom Dooley, who really helped me get back to cricket — when a lot of people thought I had no chance. Tom, who's connected with Valley football club in Brisbane, gave me exercises from go to whoa, and fixed the arm, step by step.

I was picked for the 1977 tour of England, and passed a couple of fitness tests. In the Brisbane trial I thought, well, I'll go for broke here. I had a funny sort of feeling like pins and needles in the arm. I bowled really quick, and it didn't hurt at all — just the normal feeling you get at the start of every season after your first bowl. I was erratic, because my breathing wasn't right. But I bowled bloody quick, and they said okay, I could tour.

I'd never really given up hope of coming back. For quite a while I had a stainless steel pin in the shoulder. They said, 'You won't be able to lift your arm above horizontal,' but even with that pin in, I could swing the arm over. I did the whole works of exercises with it in. It amazed them. The physio told me to stop or I'd snap the pin!

I worked really hard — even harder that I had to. I made sure I did all the exercises. Dennis Lillee had gone through the same mill with his damaged back. You have to if you're going to get back. It's the only way.

So they took the pin out earlier, because they said I was going to bust it: my arm's too strong. Dr McGuire cut the shoulder exactly where it had been cut before, through the scar tissue, and I meant to get the pin off him, but I forgot. I was going to make a necklace out of it to wear when I was bowling.

The injury was front-page news —a national sporting disaster. Ray Lindwall wrote in the *Sun* that Thommo would be missed more than Dennis Lillee. With his loss, a lot of the venom would disappear from the Australian attack. 'Thommo's great asset,' Lindwall said, with an ominous touch of finality, 'was his shock value, his ability to get that ball only just short of a length to rear up at the batsman.'

Lamenting Australia's prospects in England now that Thommo seemed an unlikely starter, as for a time he was, Lindwall went on: 'I reckon plenty of Test batsmen around the world had a much happier Christmas Day when they heard of Thommo's accident.'

Thommo himself was quoted as saying that he didn't mind missing the tour of New Zealand ('I'd rather have played in the Sheffield Shield matches for Queensland') but he was still hoping to get to England. And his adviser, David Lord, stressed that the injury would not jeopardise his $633,000 contract with 4IP.

Meanwhile, back at the Memorial Hospital, the stricken cricketer was cracking jokes between shots of morphine. 'Where's the double bed?' he yelled when Cheryl paid him one of her numerous visits.

Cheryl was obviously distraught. 'It's terrible,' she said. 'I could not believe that our wonderful, wonderful honeymoon would end like this.' Did nobody ever tell her that cricket is overflowing with the unexpected?

But the poor girl could have taken comfort from one of the surgeon's remarks. 'He is so strong and fit,' he said of his patient, 'he must have a good chance of making a full recovery.'

The patient himself, propped up in bed for a 'Press conference', shoulder and arm in sling, wearing one of those white shroud-like garments, gave his visitors a wan smile and confessed he was 'not all that flash'. The doctors, he said, had predicted that all the soreness and swelling would go in ten days. And the old fighting spirit clawed its way through the alien surroundings and the aroma of disinfectant: 'I'll be back. I'm not going to quit!'

CHAPTER 8

The Lone Gunslinger

It was bad luck to have missed the matchless excitement and sense of occasion surrounding the Centenary Test match in Melbourne in March 1977, but similarly it was no joyride taking part in the tour of England which followed. Jeff Thomson satisfied the selectors at his fitness trials, but lingering doubts existed over his ability to recover completely his pre-accident form. Many of those who witnessed the collision could hardly bring themselves to expect to see the Thommo of old ever again.

Lillee was unavailable for the tour, which only placed more responsibility on his partner. Then, of course, came the explosion of the news that thirteen of the touring team had signed to play for Kerry Packer. The cricket world was in turmoil, awash with controversy, confusion and bitterness.

The first and last Tests were drawn, but the middle three were lost — heavily. Greg Chappell's team, missing Lillee, Ian Chappell and Ross Edwards, disturbed by the Packer rumpus, and opposed by a strongish England XI, came away with the worst Test record of any Australian side to play in England since 1886.

Thommo had an undistinguished run-in to the opening Test, taking only seven wickets in first-class games at 37 apiece. He also bagged his first 'pair', against Somerset. The spring was wet, so wet that the Australians seemed to be playing more soccer than cricket. Yet their 'Wild Bull of the Pampas' was gradually working to top gear, gathering his rhythm, nipping in with the old familiar yorker, pinning fingers to bat-handles, buzzing lifters past batsmen's ears. His five wickets against MCC at Lord's gave everyone some heart, and by the time the Jubilee Test came round, Thommo was not far short of his old self.

England's new captain, Mike Brearley, who had taken over when Tony Greig was stripped of the responsibility because of his Packer allegiance, won the toss and batted, and in the fifth over Thommo struck. He beat Dennis Amiss, who nicked the ball into his stumps. It was the last ball of the over. With the first ball of his next he bounced one awkwardly at Brearley, who fended to Richie Robinson at short leg and was caught.

Derek Randall came in to face the hat-trick, and Thommo, looking even more free-flowing than usual in his short-sleeved shirt, came hurtling in. The ball was wide of the stumps and Randall left it alone.

It was a good start, but there was much hard work ahead, and by the time England had mustered 216 (Thomson 4 for 41) and Australia had gone to a lead of 80, thanks to Chappell, Serjeant and Walters, the stage was set for resistance, this time from Bob Woolmer, the sight of whose 'arse' Thommo had become so sick of two years previously at The Oval, and Tony Greig. The Kent man made 120 and the deposed captain 91.

Again Thommo had managed an early breakthrough, bowling the wretched Amiss in the first over for a duck. It was a long time before he got his next wicket, Randall, also for a duck, and two tailenders gave him four for the second time in the match, a worthy return to Test cricket.

Australia saw out the match to a draw, finishing 6 for 114, and Jeff Thomson, her ace bowler, had come through, as his captain put it, 'with much credit and little soreness'.

After bowling 23 overs in the match against Nottinghamshire, Thommo had some after-effects and was advised to rest when he saw a specialist in London. But he was ready for the second Test, at Old Trafford, where he bowled with some fire, beating Brearley with pace . . . and McCosker at slip as well. Fortunately for Australia the rebounding catch finished in the hands of Greg Chappell alongside.

Later in the innings, as Woolmer moved halfway towards yet another century, Rick McCosker put him down off Thommo, and this time there was no one to gather in the rebound. 'The General' was having a torrid time of it in the slips.

There was further frustration as England went on to 437, passing Australia's 297 with relative ease, and Thommo's spirits slumped along with his teammates. One of the biggest setbacks was when he bounced one at Tony Greig, who tried to withdraw his bat but got a touch through to Rod Marsh. The umpire heard nothing and was shielded from a sight of the touch by Greig's upper body. The Australians, especially Marsh, showed their bitter disgust.

He picked up two wickets later, Geoff Miller caught between a defensive parry and a limp hook and spooning the ball to Marsh, and Alan Knott slashing and being caught 45 yards away at third man; but he contributed to Australia's shoddy fielding performance by dropping Old at mid-on, and the touring side were relieved to get back to the dressing-room.

Monday brought more calamity and Australia were shot out for 218, Underwood taking 6 for 66, though the century made by Greg Chappell was one of the most attractive ever seen at the Manchester ground. As if he had decided to cast his cares aside and bat as if in a club match, he went for his shots and looked truly among the finest batsmen the game had seen.

England needed only 79 to win, but that evening Thommo bowled with a conviction that seemed to say 'We can win this!' The heads of

England's openers, Dennis Amiss, wearing only a cap, and Mike Brearley, with his curious pink skull-protector and chest-pad, were threatened like a pair of eggs perilously perched near the egg-poacher in the kitchen. It seemed only a matter of time before one was cracked. But they dodged dexterously, and finished at eight without loss.

I remember that evening, back at the hotel, that Jeff Thomson took me to task over that book again: *The Fast Men.* 'You say here that I only bowled at ninety!'

I referred him to a passage further on, where his 99.688 mph at Perth in 1975 is mentioned. He grinned. 'Anyway, in the morning I'll be bowling at a bloody hundred and twenty!'

And he possibly did. Except that no one was there to measure his speed accurately. Running off an exceptionally long run-up — twenty-five paces — he flung down some sizzlers. Some were short and reared, some were only just less than full-length . . . and reared. Brearley and Amiss stood their ground, Amiss in what he must have realised was his final Test appearance after his prolonged run of failures, and the captain in a determined attempt to be there when the winning runs were scored, and flicking a calculated uppercut occasionally to send the ball whirring to third man.

Mike Brearley, who steadfastly and shrewdly refuses to watch a fast bowler throughout his long run-up for fear of being mesmerised, often hums to ease the tension. His favourite theme is a cello passage from the Rasoumoffsky Quartets. As for his attitude towards facing high speed, he expressed it perfectly in his book on the 1977 series: 'Broken marriages, conflicts of loyalty, the problems of everyday life fall away as one faces up to Thomson.'

The third Test, at Trent Bridge, was where Geoff Boycott came back to Test cricket after his self-imposed exile. He made 107 and 80 not out in England's seven-wicket victory, but the course of events hung on a slips catch: Boycott had struggled for three hours in his comeback innings to reach 20 when he edged Pascoe to McCosker at second slip, and the chance was put down.

All this came later, however, for the Nottingham Test will be remembered almost as vividly for Jeff Thomson's 'heroic', 'noble', 'honourable' decision to tear up his Packer contract. He did this just before the Test began, and when he came out to bat just before tea on the first day of the match he was given a tumultuous reception by the crowd. He might almost have been a prisoner-of-war escaped from the enemy, so warm and appreciative was the applause. He explains the background to his decision:

I pulled out during the Trent Bridge Test because 4IP said I had to or else. David Lord, who'd set himself up as my 'manager', had a lot to say about things at the time, but my pulling out of Packer cricket had nothing whatever to do with him. That's what shits me, when people thought he'd organised it all. Anybody would think he was my manager and my father and sole adviser. 'Lordy' had nothing to do with me pulling out; it was strictly between World Series Cricket, Radio Station 4IP, and myself.

Frank Gardiner came over to England, acting on behalf of 4IP. He told me that was it, or else. So I had to pull out. World Series understood. They were a little bit more understanding than the Board later on when I wanted to leave Test cricket. Fortunately, they let me out of the final month of the contract so I could play in the West Indies with WSC. In July 1977 World Series could have put pressure on me and made me stay, because they'd paid me money.

David Lord had been handling some of my affairs at that time — in a mediocre sort of way. But after a while I began to realise that there was a lot of money that could have been made, and it wasn't being made. Our 'partnership' fizzled out by mutual agreement. He did a lot of good for me early on. He got me on the road, as far as publicity went. We had a fairly good time. I can't knock it. But he had *nothing* to do with me pulling out of World Series.

When Lordy and I split up, he was paid up fully. He'd helped set up the original 4IP contract, which was reckoned to be worth $633,000 to me over ten years, but later on this was modified, shortened. The new contract was worth $20,000 for three years plus my other earnings on top. I had to put up with a fair drop just to stay with them after they put the screws on me. This is what I tried to bring out in court. I'd actually put myself into debt to stay with Australian Cricket Board cricket.

That much-publicised $63,000 a year was an inflated figure anyway. The actual amount of cash that I would have received from them was probably about $28,000 I think (before tax). What with the money I lost after the busted shoulder against Pakistan, this all led to conflict. I put myself out to stay with the Board. This is the ironic part about it. Staying with the Board got me into trouble and now I wanted to get myself out of financial trouble they blocked my way, which is something I'll find hard ever to forgive them for.

When I didn't feel like going on the Test tour to the West Indies, 4IP came in again and said, You'll have to go, or the contract's not on. No option again. I had to go on the tour against my will. It was bloody ridiculous, forcing a bloke to go over there to play cricket and expecting him to do well because of their contract up there. No wonder I pulled out of the 4IP contract as soon as I could.

When I got back from the tour I went to see Frank Gardiner and told him I'd had enough and wanted to go to World Series. Frank nearly fell off the chair. Station 2SM had taken over 4IP, formed a company, but the company wasn't registered at the time, so the new contract wasn't valid. Frank found that by searching. So we said, See ya later, boys! It was a lucky break, and I was free.

The first thing I did was get in touch with Lenny Pascoe. I rang him from my parents' home in Bankstown, and Lenny rang World Series

Cricket, and they soon rang me back. They wanted to come out that same afternoon. I said, Hang on a minute; I've got stuff to do. So they were out there next morning, three of them, Andrew Caro, Austin Robertson, and one of the WSC solicitors.

The World Series contract was signed subject to 4IP letting me go, but before long I got a phone call from Board chairman Bob Parish, asking who I was going to play with. I said I was still with them, which was fair enough, because at that time 4IP said they weren't going to let me go. So the contracts with WSC were no good. I then retired from Test cricket. I sent a letter in to the Board. About the same time, Bob Simpson had sent a letter in too, saying *he* was retiring. The Board let him go nice and freely, but they knocked me on the head. They said 'No way'.

People have asked me since whether the Board did this because they suspected I was going to World Series. Well, they weren't to know where I was going. And what if Simmo had gone over? He could've if they were after him. I'd like to have seen what would've happened then.

I don't know whether they guessed about me. All I know is that I'd given the Board extra service. I'd actually suffered financially to play for them. Now I'd had enough of being behind the eight-ball. It was time to get in and make some money while I still could. I really worked during that winter, when I got back from the West Indies, training hard to make sure I was right for World Series Cricket, just waiting for the day I could bowl again in competitive cricket.

When the whole thing came to court, one of the things that came up was what I'd said to various journalists during that period. I was asked if it was true that I told one journo one thing and something different to another. Well, why should I have to tell a reporter what I'm doing? What business is it of his? I told reporters anything to get rid of them. The phone was ringing sometimes all bloody day. It drives you crazy. I'd made a gentleman's agreement that I wasn't going to tell anyone anything, anyway. Why should I have to break my promise? There's a few clowns around in the newspaper world. They'd get anything for sensationalism, but they find out in the long run that by writing bull instead of doing the right thing by us, they bugger themselves up. I don't know why they do it. Over and over again. They make it hard for the other blokes. You don't trust anybody in the end. At one stage I wouldn't speak on the phone to anybody. I didn't care who rang up. I just told them I had nothing to say, and to go to buggery, and hung up.

The questioning and meddling from Pressmen and outsiders was just as much a nuisance in those turbulent days in 1977, for not only was Thommo suddenly the favourite with *everyone* who resented the Packer 'intrusion', but he seemed possibly to be the first of a stream of defectors who had had second thoughts. Many suspected that the contracts were not binding, and that it would only take the reversals of

Thomson and Kallicharran (and Viv Richards was also said to be considering backing out), and there could be a mass walkout.

What was not generally understood was that none of the others had such a compelling financial reason as Thommo for returning to 'legitimate' cricket.

A word here about David Lord. He appeared on BBC television during the Trent Bridge Test and told viewers that Jeff Thomson had followed his conscience in withdrawing from World Series. Thommo was watching the screen in the dressing-room, and had to be restrained. 'Turn that garbage off!' he bellowed. His tour contract prevented him from making any public statement. Frank Gardiner was his guiding star, and skipper Greg Chappell a patient listener as his key fast bowler kept him abreast of developments.

I spoke with David Lord in Sydney just over a year after the Trent Bridge sensation. He had seen very little of Thommo since the 1977 tour, but still had strong feelings about their association.

'I was always a great believer in Thommo's ability — especially after coming up against him and Pascoe when Mosman played Bankstown. I take no credit for what he did out there on the field, but I do for managing his affairs — taking calls from the Press and public at all hours.'

How did Lord help him in the early days?

'It started off small, but one deal netted him a few hundred bucks. I suggested he ought to try Queensland, and when the time came I tidied up his 4IP contract. At first he was to get ten grand a year for two years plus a car. I had further discussions with Ken Mulcahy and eventually the $633,000 deal emerged. Because of Thommo's track record it was set on an aggregate basis so that he got most towards the end of the ten years. Within two months he was in trouble with the 4IP management because of his own irresponsibility. The only time in his life when he showed courage was when he suffered those two serious injuries. He was irresponsible in business.

'He used to ring me whenever he was in trouble, but he never advised Ken Mulcahy or myself when he was getting into the business of the sports shops.

'I accepted his explanation about getting into World Series early in 1977 because I understood the pressure he was under and the need for secrecy.'

To return to the Trent Bridge Test, another memorable incident was the run-out of Derek Randall. Playing before his home crowd in a Test match for the first time, the jittery hero of the Melbourne Centenary match joined Boycott after Woolmer, England's second wicket, had fallen to Pascoe without scoring. They took the total to 52, at which point Boycott played Thommo back along the pitch, just to the on side, and took off for a run.

Randall naturally hesitated, for the bowler quickly checked his follow-through and darted across to field the ball. Boycott was well and truly committed, so Randall set out for the distant far wicket, where Marsh crouched, yelling for the ball.

The aspect of the run-out that most took the eye was the way that Thommo, having picked up cleanly, flicked the ball casually, almost flippantly, to the wicketkeeper by means of a reverse arm movement. Randall was out, the crowd booed, and Boycott held his head in distress.

England were to slip to 5 for 82 before Alan Knott came in to liven things up with a sparkling century in a record-equalling sixth-wicket stand of 215 with Boycott. McCosker made a century in the second knock, but England got home on the final afternoon by seven wickets, and Australia needed to win both the remaining Tests to retain the Ashes. Thommo, now the darling of the Establishment, had three wickets and four missed chances to show for his 47 fast overs in the match.

Before the fourth Test, at Leeds, the Australians managed to lose for the first time ever to Minor Counties, and Thommo, having missed that humiliation, played in the Lancashire match, which was won.

But for a TCCB ruling directed at overseas players, Thommo might well have joined Lancashire for the 1979 season. Anxious to play again after a longish absence and keen to earn some money (about $30,000 a season), he was prepared to sign for three years. Cheryl would have accompanied him and taken on modelling work in London. But, keen as the county were to sign him up after the sacking of West Indian Colin Croft, the move was blocked by the 'November 1978' regulation whereby any overseas player not already on a county's books or verifiably already in negotiation before November 1978 was not allowed to play for the county if it already had another overseas-born player.

By the start of the World Series tour of West Indies Thommo had redesigned his future, the main aim being to get back into the Australian Test side for 1979-80. Young New South Wales speedster Geoff Lawson, playing in the Lancashire League, was tipped to join Lancashire when, out of the blue, Mick Malone, the Western Australian who had played in one Test match during the 1977 tour of England and subsequently for World Series, signed a two-year contract, taking the county of Cardus back to the days when it had top Aussie fast bowler Ted McDonald on its books half a century ago.

During the 1977 tour Thommo had had a serious offer to play county cricket. It came from much farther south, from Surrey, and he took a long time to make his mind up. Eventually, in the New Year, 1978, he turned Surrey down, having talked it over with the 4IP people. The greatest fear was that he would become bored stiff with day-after-day cricket and that it would shorten his career. Rodney Hogg expressed the same fears in January 1979 when Lancashire were trying to tempt him after a knock-back from Dennis Lillee.

When Thommo was on the market again early in 1979, Surrey were interested at first, but — before the November 1978 ruling was imposed — they broke off negotiations, probably remembering Thommo's snub to their 1977 offer. It was almost certainly a mercy, for to bowl on the slow, low pitches of Kennington Oval for a living would have been like allowing Billy the Kid only blanks for his gun. Any Australian who played in the 1975 Test match there grows fatigued at the very recollection of it.

There was nothing wrong with the Headingley wicket, and Thommo struck straightaway, getting the England captain, Brearley, caught by Rod Marsh before a run had been made. The ball swung late and was much too good for the batsman, who still had traces of Zen theory in his mind, as propounded by the German philosopher Herrigel in a book Brearley had been reading the night before. There is no record of how Thommo spent the eve of the Test, but it was a million to one on something other than Zen studies.

He bowled well that day, but it belonged to Geoff Boycott. In front of his home crowd he worked his way to his hundredth century, a deed received with enormous acclaim. Yet before lunch he survived a close call for caught-behind off Pascoe, irritating the Australians by rubbing his forearm before the umpire have his verdict.

After lunch Thommo got rid of the smooth Woolmer, caught at slip by Greg Chappell, but there was another 'incident' during the afternoon when Ray Bright thought he had Boycott caught down the leg side by Marsh. The bearded Victorian spinner lost his cool for a while and had to be spoken to by umpire Bill Alley and consoled by Greg Chappell.

After tea Thommo struck again, bowling Tony Greig with one that cut back. But all was soon forgotten in the hysteria that greeted Boycott's hundred, and at the end of the day England were 4 for 252.

Twenty-four hours later Australia were halfway to ruin. England climbed up to 436 (Thomson 4 for 113 from 34 overs) and by the end Australia were five down for 67. The Ashes were slipping through their fingers. Two wickets each to Hendrick and Botham and the tragic run-out of McCosker by Randall as he backed up too far broke the back of the innings, and if Thommo looked to the far side of the ground he would have seen a banner proclaiming: 'Ashes to ashes, dust to dust, bionic Thommo's turned to rust!' How attitudes had changed in a mere two years.

On the third day he put the first half of his 'pair' in the book, bowled by a Botham leg-cutter second ball, and Australia's misery was complete with a total of 103, their lowest ever at Headingley.

So they followed on, and by the fourth evening it was all over — defeat by an innings. All England was alive with celebration. It was a lonely time for the Australians.

Thommo had the 'distinction' of becoming Bob Willis's hundredth Test wicket, bowled second ball for nought after playing a no-ball, and his 'pair' was a sombre gift for his twenty-seventh birthday next day.

The three-nil drubbing, to be followed by an even bigger beating in the 1978-79 series to follow, left Jeff Thomson and all his team-mates — whether they played in the Tests or not — with a burning desire to straighten the record at the next opportunity.

After an unimpressive showing against Middlesex at Lord's, the Australians saddled up for the final Test, at The Oval. The first day was lost to rain but on the second they came back by dismissing England for 214, Thommo taking 4 for 87 (three bowled and one lbw) and Mick Malone, on Test debut, taking 5 for 63 off 47 overs.

The match was drawn, Australia taking a first-innings lead of 171 and taking two England wickets in the remaining overs, Thommo's capture of Brearley's wicket (caught at short leg off the splice of the bat) raising his total for the series to a creditable 23, at 25.34. He had bowled fast throughout, but relatively speaking he was not as rapid as the Englishmen of 1974-75 had known him, and he had almost completely forsaken the bouncer.

The greatest pleasure for him at The Oval was his hundredth Test wicket. It was in his 22nd Test match, and he remembers it well:

One of the highlights for me was when I took my hundredth Test wicket. One of the Pressmen had pointed out when I was on 99, and we'd just taken the new ball. I can remember as plain as day the ball that did it. It was pretty useful — fast, and jagged back. Graham Roope was nowhere and it bowled him. I never set out to have any goals like that, but it was very satisfying, a hundred Test wickets. I thought at the time, Well, that's enough for me.

I came across a magazine article once that listed all the fast-bowling pairs, and it had those fellas who bowled against Bradman — Larwood and Voce — at the top for the most successful partnership. And Dennis and I came next, above Roberts and Holding. For the top striking rates for fast bowlers individually, you know, a wicket every so many balls, well I had the best of the lot, by a long way. I just picked the magazine up in the newsagent's. It was really interesting.

Okay, so Ian Botham has beaten those figures and got his hundred Test wickets faster than anyone else, but he's been playing against blokes who are very ordinary if you ask me. I'd say he gets most of his wickets in England, where it does a bit.

As far as touring goes, one of the drags is social functions. You get hangers-on and people who bore you to death, but I think I've always managed to turn it on for them okay. I think while I was with 4IP I did it as well as anyone could do it. I really mean that. Even though it really wasn't me. I'd rather talk to somebody who's going to benefit from it than some bloke who comes up to you and wants to talk to you just so he can tell his mates that he knows Jeff Thomson. That gives me the horrors. But it's something I've had to put up with. I've had a couple of run-ins, but I don't bother arguing with the aggressive ones. If somebody really got on my goat I'd soon let 'em know! If they're not interested in you, perhaps that's the time to start worrying!

As for autographs, if kids are keen on you, it doesn't take much to sign an autograph. It's not much time out of your life.

He'd signed his share of autographs on the tour and taken all of his share of wickets, second only to Bob Willis in the series for either side. Perhaps the figure which counted most, though, was that in his fourteen Tests against England to date he had taken 72 wickets — a mighty performance.

If his reputation as a killer bowler had been dimmed slightly during this unhappy tour, he was at least still on people's minds — not least the selectors', who were faced with the prospect of keeping him in trim as the spearhead bowler against India and in West Indies in the season immediately following. It was in the minds of administrators both in England and Australia to outlaw the World Series players, and it seemed at that time that never again would Lillee and Thomson share the attack for their country in Test cricket. It was a troublesome time.

EMI had cut a record by Richard Stilgoe in the spring, before Lillee's decision to miss the English tour had been announced. The disc was entitled, predictably, 'Lillian Thomson', and, playing heavily on the word 'bouncers', lyricised how 'She hit Randall on the ankle then she hit him on the forehead; if she finds the happy medium she could hurt him something horrid.'

Injuries to English batsmen during this 1977 series were very few and far between, making the previous Ashes series in Australia seem more than ever like something out of Scotland Yard's Black Museum.

Another record harmonised proudly: 'We've got Thommo, Thommo — he knows what bowling's all about.' It went on: 'Howzat, you hear the people shout.' And it finished with reference to 'Pommies on the skids.' That, for the moment, was an outdated sentiment.

CHAPTER 9

Indian Magic

And so to the season that broke his spirit, when he missed his mates more than he could bear, and when the depressing experience of playing with a weakened Test side got the better of him.

For Queensland he again delivered the goods, taking 32 wickets at 20.46, which, with Geoff Dymock's 41 at 24.78 and David Ogilvie's sensational 1060 Shield runs, with six centuries, took Queensland to the now-familiar runners-up spot. With greater depth of talent they might have pulled off the Sheffield Shield, but it was not to be.

The Indian team arrived, with Bishan Bedi, the captain, and all his players well aware of their responsibility to Test cricket in the face of the challenge of the first series of Kerry Packer cricket, with its massive publicity build-up. The Australian Board's master-stroke was to persuade 41-year-old Bobby Simpson out of retirement to captain the Test side, after ten years away from Test cricket.

He was in trim as far as continuous club cricket had permitted, but the first ventures back into the first-class cricket arena were not without difficulties. Before his first Shield game he led New South Wales against Queensland at the Gabba in a Gillette Cup match, and made 28 not out in a six-wicket victory. But Thommo beat him for speed several times in the eleven balls he whipped down at him. He said he had batted like 'an old woman', but the signs were there that he could defeat the lost years and hold his own against the top opposition again once he'd got the feel of it. In the opening Test match he made 89 and put everyone's mind at rest.

It was a thrilling game, won by Australia by 16 runs, just what the loyalist public wanted. And Thommo took seven wickets while his new partner, Wayne Clark, took eight. So far so good. Thommo also made a valuable 41 not out in the second innings — a performance that could be seen at the end as having much to do with Australia's win.

His stand of 50 for the last wicket with Alan Hurst, who made 26, made India's task that little bit more demanding — and also gave the crowd some grand entertainment, for Thommo hoisted Chandrasekhar onto the greyhound track and then flat-batted Madan Lal into the members' bar.

The pitch didn't offer much to the pace bowlers, but Thommo still had the batsmen on edge. He secured a rare 'hit wicket' victim in the first innings when Dilip Vengsarkar jerked quickly out of the way of a vicious bouncer and lost his cap, which fell on the stumps.

In the second innings, after taking some of his team-mates fishing on the rest day, Thommo got Amarnath, caught behind by Steve Rixon, little Viswanath, brilliantly caught in the gully by Ogilvie, and then Patel, leg-before to a very fast near-yorker. But Thommo was running out of steam, as was Wayne Clark. India crept nearer their target.

Sunil Gavaskar, having come back from a three-week lay-off through a leg injury, made a fine century, but after he was seventh out and Madan Lal soon followed, Kirmani and Bedi took the score past 300. It was becoming a cliffhanger.

Only 23 runs were needed when Kirmani, having made 55, was caught when pulling Hurst to midwicket. And then Thommo completed the execution six runs later by having Chandrasekhar, perhaps the easiest victim in Test cricket, caught low and in his fingertips by 'keeper Rixon.

Man of the Match was Peter Toohey for his innings of 82 and 57, but the overall winner was Test cricket, and those who supported it breathed deep sighs of relief.

Yet it was no time to dispense with the nerve tablets, for there was another thriller coming up in Perth. The second Test was won by two wickets, and poor old India, contributing well enough to the excitement of this all-important series, began to wonder if they would ever win a Test on Australian soil.

It was a petrifyingly hot day, with the temperature around 40°C, and India had the good fortune to bat and make 329 for the loss of seven by stumps. The Australian bowlers were called upon for a gutsy display, and none responded more courageously than Thommo, who took four of the wickets, the fourth after tea with the new ball after he had been in agony with leg cramps.

'That's what I'm here for!' he is said to have told his skipper when asked if he could use the new ball.

Bob Simpson showed all the skill and tenacity of his early days in making 176 as Australia replied to India's 402 with 394. Having taken his hundredth Test catch, he now recorded his ninth Test century, and middle-aged cricketers everywhere threw their chests out with pride. Thommo cursed his luck when a massive hit off Venkataraghavan which would have been six on many grounds ended up in Amarnath's hands, and he had his eighth Test duck.

Now back to the serious business, and this time India called the tune, piling up 240 runs before the second wicket fell. Gavaskar and Amarnath made centuries, the latter following his 90 in the first innings, but wickets fell rapidly after that, and with nine down, Bedi declared at 330 after Thommo had hit his valuable spin bowler Chandrasekhar on the boot with what he likes to term his 'Sandshoe Crusher'.

Three hundred and thirty-nine to win in six-and-a-half hours: a formidable task against the famed Indian spinners, even if the pitch was still playing well. John Dyson was out that evening, and at the start of the last day Australia wanted 314 in six hours. That they got them owed a great deal to Tony Mann, the spin bowler sent in as night-watchman. The left-hander clumped his way to an incredible century, with Toohey making 83 and Ogilvie 47 (leaving Mann to score 94 of the 139 they added for the third wicket). It was an historic victory, and to Thommo fell the honour of making the winning hit, a big drive over mid-off from the second ball of the third-last over, with Wayne Clark his partner and only Sam Gannon to follow.

The series was shaping up like that series of sensations in 1960-61 when Australia and West Indies caused so many lost heartbeats.

India's day of triumph came at Melbourne in the third Test, where Chandrasekhar, the magical fast-medium leg-spin/top-spin/googly bowler, took six wickets in each innings and Gavaskar scored yet another century.

Thommo inflicted a duck on Gavaskar at the start of the match as he tried to hook and was caught at the wicket down the leg side. He took two further wickets, but was hampered by a slightly strained hamstring muscle and was off the field later in the innings.

In reply to India's modest 256 Australia made only 213, most of the runs coming from Craig Serjeant (85) and Gary Cosier (67). Thommo, not enjoying one of his better Tests, was a Chandrasekhar victim without scoring, caught in the outfield again, second ball.

Now, would India let it slip? They didn't. Gavaskar's 118 steered them towards a second-innings total of 343. Thommo bowled, but not at full speed, and the ball was greasy from the rain on the rest day. New Year's Day brought little joy for Australia.

When Gavaskar and Co. had finished their task Australia needed 387 to win the match and the series. They were all out for 164.

Bhagwat Chandrasekhar, the shy man from Karnataka, was Man of the Match for his 12 for 104, but the little master, Gavaskar, made a vital contribution to India's historic victory. And as a student of the game he later had views on Jeff Thomson's bowling that warrant repetition:

'Thommo is the fastest bowler I've faced,' Gavaskar wrote in India's *Cricket Quarterly* magazine. 'In fact, there are just one or two spells from other bowlers which have come anywhere near his speed. Like John Price's fiery overs at Old Trafford in 1971; Dennis Lillee's at Perth the same year and Michael Holding's at Jamaica. But for sheer speed over a series I've never faced anyone quicker. Most fast bowlers like to tell you what you should expect from the next ball, but not Thomson.'

Gavaskar got to know him well enough to sum up the man like this: 'He likes to sit by himself in the dressing-room, hardly exchanging small talk with anybody. He is, I think, a simple, honest man who because of his powerful shoulder earned fame and became the idol of millions of cricket-lovers all over the world. There's nothing he would like better to do than to get away from it all, maybe go fishing with cans of beer by his side.'

No fishing for the moment, however, for there was a job to do — like beating off the Indian challenge.

Yet at Sydney, in the fourth Test, the touring side had another resounding win, this time by an innings, to draw level two-all in the series. Chandrasekhar and Bedi demolished Australia for 131. India were already 86 without loss that first evening.

Six Indians passed 40 as the lead was stretched to 265 before Bedi declared with eight down. Thommo had again done his stuff and was so very clearly Australia's heavy gun. While he operated, India could never relax. When he rested, it looked more like a club match. This time he took 4 for 83 off 27 overs, having Gavaskar caught, hooking, for 49, knocking two of Viswanath's stumps out of the ground, forcing Mankad to play on, and jumping one at Ghavri, who parried it to gully. On top of this he had Vengsarkar missed at slip by Simpson — a catch he would have pocketed with ease in his younger days.

Cosier and Toohey made runs in the second innings, but the rain stayed away for India to clinch victory by an innings and two runs on the final morning, Toohey falling to an unbelievable catch by Madan Lal at fine leg.

Australian sports-followers were worried now. Many of them didn't see their Test team as the 'golden youngsters' any more, the 'bright hopes for the future', the 'welcome new faces'. They were a bunch of no-hopers, and Test cricket wasn't what it used to be. The Packer stars should be brought back. Simmo was too old. What wouldn't Lillee and the Chappells and Hookesy and Marsh do to this Indian mob?

Patience, traditionally in short ration on the Hill at Sydney and in the Southern Stand at Melbourne, had shrunk to a frazzle.

Five changes were made. Out went Dyson, Serjeant, Hughes, Mann and Gannon. In came Graeme Wood, Rick Darling, Graham Yallop, Bruce Yardley and Ian Callen. It worked. But only just.

Australia seemed in an impregnable position after making 505, Yallop hitting his first-ever Test century and Simpson his second of the series. The new openers, Wood and Darling, had begun well with 89, and progress had been made all along the line, Thommo and Callen putting on 47 for the last wicket and raising the half-thousand.

Then came the sensational start to the Indian innings early on the second afternoon. Thommo let a full-toss slip and Gavaskar stroked it to the cover boundary. The score moved on to 23. Then three wickets fell . . . and Australia lost her ace bowler.

The first wicket came when Thommo rasped a short one at Gavaskar, who could only fend it to Toohey at gully. Then Amarnath jabbed another lifter to short leg, where Cosier scooped up a catch which did not appear to everybody to be clean. Nevertheless, Amarnath had to go, and still at 23, Chauhan hit Clark into midwicket's hands. Three casualties without a run added.

Then, halfway through his fourth over, Thommo suddenly pulled up in his run-up, clutching his leg. It was the hamstring muscle again. He left the field, to bowl no more in the match. The Adelaide jinx!

Clark and Callen got rid of India for 269, and Simpson didn't enforce the follow-on, despite a lead of 236, hoping Thomson would recover and knowing that it would be easier facing the Indian spinners now rather than on a worn fifth- and sixth-day pitch.

Darling made another half-century, as did Simpson, and with Australia all out 256, India needed 493 for victory, with over fourteen hours left — and no Thommo to bowl at them.

They came dramatically close. Having made 406 to beat West Indies by six wickets at Port of Spain two years previously, it might not have been such an enormous surprise if they had pulled off this staggering requirement at Adelaide. But they made 445 and fell by 47 runs. It was a fitting climax for Simpson — who took the final wicket on this his forty-second birthday — and for the bunch of newcomers who had given the Australian cricket public its money's worth.

As for the averages, Jeff Thomson was top for Australia, with 22 wickets at 23.45, only Wayne Clark having taken more: 28. So much for playing at home against a fair batting side with plenty of spin. bowling. Now for an away series that threatened much greater hardships at the hands of the West Indian fast bowling and power batting.

CHAPTER 10

Caribbean Hardships

When Jeff Thomson was appointed vice-captain of Australia for the tour of West Indies early in 1978, under Bobby Simpson's leadership, he was a proud man. He was even seen wearing a tie to net practice, and in his enthusiasm he went out and bought a stylish, powder-blue, lightweight suit to wear during the tour. Frank Gardiner recalls seeing it upon his return, and complimenting him on it. 'Yeah,' said Thommo, 'I bought the f------ thing to wear in the West Indies, but the bloody Board wouldn't let me wear it. I had to wear their stupid bloody schoolboy's uniform all the time!'

The tour was an unhappy episode in the lives of Thommo and many of his team-mates. He claimed he was used as a workhorse by Simpson, though he bowled only 151.2 overs in the five Test matches and a mere 35 overs in the three other first-class matches in which he played. At times he was lively enough to rival any of the much-vaunted West Indian speedsters, but often he lacked zip — the effect of psychological rather than physical inertia. He hadn't got the bowling support he'd been used to, and he wilted. First Lillee had missed the tour of England; then Pascoe, Walker and Malone had gone to the World Series camp. Wayne Clark tried hard, but by the fifth Test he was out with an injury, as was Ian Callen, and Thommo found himself opening the bowling for Australia with medium-pacer Trevor Laughlin.

He explains some of the causes of his irritation:

I said at the end of the 1977 tour of England that we often played like a bunch of schoolkids. And it was sometimes like that in the West Indies. Just imagine how a bloke'd feel when there's a very simple run-out on, like in the second Test, in Bridgetown, when all Bruce Yardley had to do was underarm the ball to me and the guy was run out by miles. But he threw the bloody thing over my head. I just couldn't believe it. We needed a win more than anything against these blokes, and that would've been nice and handy. I lost my cool and I kicked the stumps over and I just glared at him I reckon for a minute at least. That's when the crowd started giving me a razz after that. They didn't quite understand. Anyway, I decided I'd give them a razz. I shouldn't have done what I did, but it was all in the heat of the game.

The crowd were cranky with me for a while. It sometimes takes me a while to cool down. There was a photo of me with my hand raised, apparently waving to two people!

I enjoyed having a bit of authority on that tour, as vice-captain. It was a bit of an experience. We never lost any of the games where I skippered. I didn't do so much bowling in the games where I was captain. It may sound like I was dodging some of the work, but we'd had a hard series against India, and I reckoned I needed nursing a bit. I'd done a lot of work against the Indians, and you get sick and tired of doing it on your own.

Pitches in the West Indies just don't suit fast bowling. Okay, Garner and Croft got wickets in Trinidad, but the wicket was wet. It was unbelievable. The ball would pitch six feet in front of the batsman and go way over his head, or smash him in the hands as he tried to protect himself. It dried out next day and was as flat as a Pakistan pitch. The West Indians didn't bowl too badly.

Our blokes batted terribly against them. To be honest, they looked frightened. I don't care what anyone says — they looked apprehensive. Which annoyed me. That's where those blokes got on top to start with. I might have been apprehensive myself, but that didn't stop me from trying, and getting behind them. I might have got out, but it was only through my lack of ability — not lack of guts.

I hung in there with Yardley in Bridgetown when he made his 70-odd, and we put 55 together for the eighth wicket, of which I made 12. That evening I whipped out Gordon Greenidge, Viv Richards and Kallicharran. Not a bad day's work.

Something that annoyed me was the way Bob Simpson sometimes bowled himself before Higgs and Yardley, who were spin specialists. It was all right in selections. We all had a fair bit of say. But on the field there wasn't much consultation. I can't complain. And I don't blame Simmo for how badly we went. I blame the guys for not pulling their fingers out. It was like a fight when a bloke's throwing punches at you and you're not throwing any back. You can't do that. You've got to get into 'em. That's exactly what they didn't do, and that's why we went bad to start with.

Admittedly these West Indians were top players, these World Series blokes we were up against. But you can still put up a fight.

I couldn't care less about this World Series players and Board players business. That was all crap. It was Australia playing against West Indies. They're all players, playing for their country — the best team available. That's how it should be.

I lost a lot of heart when Clive Lloyd and the other World Series players pulled out of the West Indies Test team. I wasn't then playing against the best West Indian side any longer. I lost a lot of drive. I kept thinking to myself, we're just playing against a lot of second-raters now. I didn't go well after that. I took nine wickets in the first two Tests in two and a bit innings, and in the three Tests after that I only took eleven wickets in six innings. I got turned right off. I tried to stop it, but it was just something that was there, because I wasn't playing against the world's best. That's why I went over to World Series Cricket.

There's no future in playing if your heart's not there. I had to go where it was. This is it, I thought. I've had it.

I'd never had an alternative to consider before, until Kerry Packer came along.

The first two Tests were lost heavily against the full might of West Indies, World Series players and all. But when Desmond Haynes, Richard Austin and Deryck Murray were dropped for the third Test, captain Clive Lloyd resigned, and his exit was quickly followed by the rest of the World Series players. The reshaped team, led by Alvin Kallicharran, lost the Test, but won the fourth, to clinch the series, and the fifth and final Test was abandoned after a crowd disturbance when West Indies, 111 runs from victory with only one wicket standing, had 6.2 overs to survive.

Thommo's minor strains during the series against India had persuaded Greg Chappell to write that 'Jeff must realise he is a little older and therefore has to work that much harder on his fitness. He can no longer rely on youthful natural fitness to pull him through.'

There were further niggling muscle problems during the tour of West Indies, and some of the Australian journalists covering the series thought that he might, with advantage, have taken more exercise, during or between matches. By the fifth Test, John Benaud was writing that Thommo's arm was low and 'gone was the lift and the slanting cut that had shattered the world's best batsmen just a month before at Bridgetown. Too many of his deliveries went way down leg-side. He looked gone.'

Fortunately it was only a brief period of lethargy. At the start of the following season he was to bowl fast and furiously in a charity match at Drummoyne Oval, spurred by the presence of Dennis Lillee at the other end — the first time they had bowled in tandem since the shoulder accident in the Adelaide Test almost two years before. By now he had signed for World Series Cricket, and fresh troubles were just round the corner.

Back at the start of the West Indies tour, his troubles centred around an errant front foot, which caused umpire Ralph Gosein to no-ball him 22 times in his ten overs in the one-day international in Antigua. After five overs of this, with 16 no-ball shouts, Thommo was threatening to bowl leg-spinners when an on-field conference began. Gosein disappeared and returned with the Laws of Cricket, which he thumbed through for Simpson's benefit. Then the contest continued, with Haynes racing to a magnificent 148 while Thommo took 4 for 67. The Australians were not disgraced against the hefty attack of Roberts, Croft, Garner and Daniel, but lost on run rate when bad light halted play.

He bowled well against Trinidad on a spinner's pitch, though he took only one wicket. But there were no no-balls this time, and the muscular discomfort which had kept him out of the opening match seemed to have vanished. A six-wicket victory put Bob Simpson and his young team in the right frame of mind for the opening Test, at Port of Spain. The frame was soon disfigured.

Simpson described the pitch as 'terrible' for the first day of a Test match. In the opening over a divot flew up, and the Australians, put in by Clive Lloyd, formed a steady procession to and from the crease. Peter Toohey took a sickening blow above the right eye from a Roberts bouncer, and bled profusely. The wound needed three stitches, but he gallantly came back later. Gary Cosier fought bravely for 46, but the innings ended for 90, and that evening West Indies were already 78 without loss.

West Indies made 405, Kallicharran a century, Lloyd 86, Haynes 61, and on the third day Australia were demolished by an innings, bowled out this time for 209, Yallop making 81.

A number of people, including Board president Jeff Stollmeyer, said the pitch ought to be dug up, and Bob Simpson complained bitterly after the match, saying that a Test should always start on a perfect wicket. This match, he said, was decided on the toss of the coin.

Thommo was one player who did not disappoint. He gave it everything, and finished with the prize wickets of Viv Richards and Clive Lloyd, as well as Richard Austin, for 84 off 21 overs (one of which actually cost him 20 runs, including a hooked six by Haynes).

He was rested during the Barbados match, drawn when Australia's disappointing bowling could make little impression in the second innings after the batsmen had secured a first-innings lead of 220. Then it was time for the second Test, when Australia had their moments.

The first day was action-packed. Australia were 105 for the loss of Rick Darling before a collapse set in and six wickets fell for 56 runs. Bruce Yardley, aided by Thommo, then smacked the ball in all directions — and took a lot of punishment himself around the legs and body. His 74 saved the day, though Simpson sought out the umpires on the matter of the number of bouncers bowled by six-foot-eight Joel Garner.

The last session was electric. Thommo bowled with all the old spark and looked to be at least as quick as anything the locals had to offer. And his duel with Viv Richards has gone down as one of the all-time great personal challenges.

The gifted West Indian was dropped at long leg off an attempted hook off Thommo, before he had scored, and reacted with an amazing hit, standing up to the bowler and sending the ball over square leg and clean into the stand. Having already accounted for Gordon Greenidge, caught off the glove, Thommo now fixed Richards, who was 23 in as many minutes. Another sizzling bouncer was top-edged to long leg and this time Clark completed the catch. And from the final ball of the day

Thommo dug one in at Kallicharran, who gave a catch to short leg. West Indies were thus 3 for 71, Thommo having taken all three wickets.

The effort caused a recurrence of leg strain, and after three overs next day he went off for treatment. But he came back later to take three more wickets and finish with 6 for 77, the best figures ever for Australia at Kensington Oval, Bridgetown.

So West Indies were only 38 ahead on the first innings. But now the match was torn from Australia's grasp as five wickets tumbled that evening for 96 to a fast attack that seemed to be under no restriction in short-pitched bowling. Bouncer after bouncer was hurled down, ramming home the realisation that against this flotilla of battleships Australia had just the one high-power cruiser. After they had reached 178 on the third day and set West Indies 141 to win, Australia flung her lone fighter at the opposition, but after six overs of honest-to-goodness speed and endeavour Thommo came off and Greenidge and Haynes romped to the brink of victory, which eventually came by nine wickets.

That made it a deficit of two Tests with three to go, and the risk of devastation by depression in morale became greater by the day. There were further setbacks in the Guyana match.

Here, Jeff Thomson captained an Australian team for the first time. He decided to spare himself, and spent the entire innings at mid-on and mid-off, to the frustration of the Bourda crowd, who had never seen him bowl. He left the bowling to Callen, Laughlin, Cosier and Yardley and gave his leg a further chance to recover.

Rick Darling and Graham Yallop made centuries on the opening day, but Yallop, who had just become the first batsman ever to bat in a Test match in a protective helmet, chose to discard it — and at 118 he was hit by a lifter from Croft and sustained a broken jaw that was to keep him out of the game for three weeks.

Cosier made a century in the second innings, but there was further disaster on the final day when Bruce Yardley was knocked cold by another Croft bouncer, and it was time for tour manager Fred Bennett to utter a protest at the umpires' laxity.

They will tell you in Lancashire that Colin Croft, the six-foot-four air traffic controller from Demarara, can perhaps become a little too interested in hitting 'Whiteys'. Certainly his length was erratic in his brief time with the county, who were eventually forced to discard him. It may be an injustice, just as the infamous 1974 interview with Thommo was open to question; but by his tactics in March 1978 it could reasonably be deduced that Croft, who took an amazing 8 for 29 against Pakistan in his first Test series, cares as little about inflicting pain on batsmen as any fast bowler in the game's long history.

Thommo decided to have a bowl in the final innings, sending down seven overs as Guyana played out time. He also had enough sense of humour to give Kim Hughes a bowl, and the Western Australian, returning after an appendix operation, took a wicket with his first ball in first-class cricket.

Now came a taste of Test success, after the strengths of the sides had been balanced by the withdrawal of the disgruntled World Series West Indians. With great pace and control, Thommo took 4 for 57 on the opening day at Georgetown, with Clark backing him well with 4 for 64. Australia, with half-centuries from Wood, Simpson and Rixon, gained a lead of 81; but then the match developed into a classic fight.

On the second evening Thommo's bowling was a lot looser, and Jamaican Basil 'Shotgun' Williams, playing in his first Test, took toll of it, and went on to his century the next day. Larry Gomes, too, made his first Test hundred, and by the time the innings ended on the third evening Australia faced a tall order: 359 for victory.

By the fourth evening they were 290 for the loss of six wickets. The first three had fallen for next to nothing, but a wonderful record stand of 251 between Graeme Wood and Craig Serjeant, both of whom made their maiden Test centuries, set up the victory. Three more wickets fell that evening, but on the final morning Steve Rixon and Trevor Laughlin added another 48 in an hour and when Laughlin was out Bruce Yardley came in to finish the job. Thommo, next man in, wasn't needed.

It was a deeply satisfying victory, especially to Bob Simpson, the veteran 'comeback' captain, who was playing first-class cricket before some of his players and opponents were born. He couldn't bring himself to watch the latter stages of the match, such was the tension.

Was this the turning-point? The team moved on to Grenada and beat Windward Islands on a poor pitch and then won the second one-day international by two wickets, Thommo scampering a single off the last possible ball.

Then it was back to earth with a thump.

On a spinning fourth-day pitch at Port of Spain, needing 293 for victory, Australia were cut down for 94 as Derek Parry took 5 for 15 and Raphick Jumadeen 3 for 34. This after having been neck-and-neck on first innings and having West Indies seven down for 204 in their second.

The match saw Thommo give one of his least impressive performances in his Test career. In 38 overs in the match he picked up just three late-order wickets and conceded 140 runs. Norbert Phillip had been rough on him when a second new ball was taken on the third day, and four overs had produced 33 runs.

A protest group had organised a boycott of the match, which never saw more than 5000 spectators on any day. Irate at the rift between the West Indies Board of Control and the Packer players, some of the protesters picketed outside the ground with placards.

Perhaps their theme got through to Thommo as well as to so many of the Trinidad populace.

Certainly the small attendances did nothing for the atmosphere of the Test match — something to which so many cricketers are susceptible. After playing in front of 80,000 at Melbourne, this must have seemed like playing a county match midweek, with only a few hundred watching. The effect on Thommo would not be too attractive.

He skippered again against Jamaica, and gave himself a rest in the second innings after two wickets in ten overs in the first. The sensation of the match — and one of the talking points of a sensational tour — was the calling of Yardley by umpire Sang Hue for throwing. The Australians were stunned.

Thommo was in at the kill as the Australians won by two wickets, defying fast bowler Michael Holding, who had taken seven wickets in his comeback match. Then, with a certain amount of relief, they faced up to the final Test match, also at Kingston. More heartache followed.

It began promisingly enough, Australia making 343, thanks to a century from Peter Toohey. West Indies replied with 280, Gomes making another century and Trevor Laughlin working hard for 5 for 101.

Australia now took command, piling up 305 for three wickets before Simpson declared, Toohey getting to within three runs of a second century in the match when he was stumped, and Graeme Wood making a confident 90. It was West Indies' turn to struggle on the fifth day.

Spinners Yardley and Higgs worked their way through the order, and though Kallicharran made a worthy 126, defeat was staring West Indies in the face as Vanburn Holder was given out caught behind off Higgs. He showed disagreement and left the field very slowly. Then the bottles began to rain onto the outfield, and pandemonium broke loose.

Somebody tried to set fire to the grandstand, the police were firing blanks, dozens of security men and police ran onto the field to protect the players, and for almost half an hour a major threat presented itself to cricketers and cricket ground alike. Everything the rioters could lay their hands on was being tossed onto the field.

Eventually the players decided to run for the relative safety of the dressing-room. Then the diplomatic row blew up. The Board suggested the remaining 6.2 overs should be played the next day, but umpire Gosein refused, pointing to the regulations, which stated that the match was to be played over five days. The West Indies manager is believed to have opposed a resumption as well, perhaps as troubled by the damage done to the pitch as any other consideration.

And in that confused and hostile manner the 1978 Australian tour of West Indies, acrimonious at almost every twist and turn, came somewhat mercifully to a close. The team had a few days in peaceful Bermuda before returning to Australia, and Thommo finished up with 3 for none against a Select XI. Little could he have guessed that, after twelve months of controversy, legal wrangles, abuse and acres of newspaper coverage of his progress, setbacks, aims and grievances, he would be back in those fair Caribbean waters, back with his old mates, playing in World Series colours . . . and enduring another riot.

CHAPTER 11

Fast, Faster, Fastest

Probably the finest book ever written on the techniques of fast bowling, what makes a fast bowler, and the training methods and injury-treatment devised by modern medical men is *The Art of Fast Bowling* by Dennis Lillee, with the assistance of Ian Brayshaw. In the book there is reference to the scientifically-conducted tests carried out on four of the world's top fast bowlers by Tom Penrose and Brian Blanksby of the University of Western Australia's Department of Physical Education, and Daryl Foster of the Secondary Teachers' College in Perth. The bowlers were Jeff Thomson, Dennis Lillee, Andy Roberts, and Michael Holding — a quartet guaranteed to have walked through many a Test batsman's nightmares.

The tests, carried out at the WACA ground during play in the Perth Test match between Australia and West Indies, were carried out through two high-speed photosonic cameras operating at selected speeds of between 200 and 400 frames a second and lined up at right-angles to the two bowling creases. The conditions were more realistic than in the nets or on a practice ground, since the bowlers were observing the necessities during an actual match of not no-balling and not bowling too loose a length or direction.

The fastest delivery measured was one of Thommo's.

It went at 160.45 km/hr (99.70 mph) from the hand and was travelling at 129.92 (80.73) as it reached the batting end. The loss of velocity was unduly high in this instance because it was a short-pitched ball. Thommo's second-fastest delivery started at 159.49 (99.10) and hit the bat at 138.40 (86.00).

Roberts, who was not quite at his best, recorded the next-best speed, Holding after him, and Lillee, who was measured faster at the University two days earlier, came in at 139.03 (86.39) release speed, 115.92 (72.03) speed at the batting end. Without question batsmen had known him faster.

It was further calculated that when Thommo let rip with his 99 mph ball, West Indian opener Roy Fredericks had 0.438 seconds to do something about it. Since tests had shown that a batsman needs a minimum of 0.30 seconds to assess a ball of that speed and to decide on a course of action, and a further 0.30 seconds to perform the stroke, there was a time deficit there of 0.162 seconds!

As for no-balls, one might have supposed that Thommo, with his notorious tendency to give them away by the handful, would often cost his side dearly. Yet with the umpire starting his shout 0.301 seconds after the front foot has landed (0.214 seconds after the release of the ball), Thommo's fastest delivery would already be halfway down the pitch before the batsman had his warning.

Among the most interesting findings in Lillee's book were the measurements of the speed of the run-up. Lillee, of the four, ran in the fastest 33.57 km/hr (20.86 mph). Roberts was next with 28.78 (17.88). Then came Holding, 28.10 (17.46). And, not surprisingly to anyone who has watched him, Thommo trotted in at a leisurely 18.02 km/hr (11.20 mph). By my reckoning that would give him a time of 20 seconds for the 100 metres, while Lillee would have a time of 10.72! This disregards the pick-up time from the start, presumably, as well as the extra distance covered by a 100-metre sprinter.

It was concluded that as Thommo and Holding pivoted over a straight front leg during delivery they gained maximum benefit from their height and achieved sharp bounce and lift off the pitch. Elsewhere there is reference to fast-contracting and slow-contracting muscle fibre — an inborn characteristic. Dr Frank Pyke, who had so much to do with Lillee's fitness, writes of Jeff Thomson's orientation towards fast-contracting muscle fibres, and says that well-muscled fast bowlers such as Thommo and Graham McKenzie would be wasting their time in strength-building programmes.

Then there is the matter of what relative importance there is in (a) the run-up, (b) leg action and hip rotation, (c) trunk flexion and shoulder girdle rotation, (d) arm action, and (e) hand flexion. Jeff Thomson, the splendid natural cricketing wild animal, would have spent even less time pondering these components than the rest of us, so busy has he been in trying to take wickets.

But the fascinating findings of Brian Blanksby and Ken Davis are: (a) 19 per cent, (b) 23 per cent, (c) 11 per cent, (d) 42 per cent, (e) 5 per cent. These figures are the result of tests on seventeen Perth club cricketers, and must serve only as broad guidelines. With Thommo's slower run-up and super-powerful shoulder action the components would need reassessment. At the end of it all, bearing in mind his performances on certain days, it would be no surprise if the sum total of the components came out at 120 per cent!

Perhaps he knew more than we would suspect way back in 1974 when he told Sydney journalist Phil Wilkins of his plans for preparing for the Poms: 'A bit of football and some gym work, not too much because it puts on muscle and muscle slows you down — and Scotch whisky instead of beer. Drink Scotch and your belly's okay, but you wake up with a sore head. That makes you good and cranky.'

Just over four years later, now a signatory of World Series Cricket, Thommo took part in a contest between a dozen of the world's top fast bowlers — and won it. He took the $4000 prize for being the fastest

(147.90 km/hr — 91.86 mph), and, somewhat unexpectedly for one with his reputation, the extra $1000 prize for accuracy too.

The 'Fastest Bowler in the World' was adjudged after eight balls filmed with a high-speed camera, the results fed into a computer. With great pride, one day he will be able to show his grandchildren the names that trailed after him on the final result sheet: Michael Holding, Imran Khan, Garth Le Roux, Colin Croft, Andy Roberts, Dennis Lillee, Wayne Daniel, Len Pascoe, Richard Hadlee, Mike Procter, Sarfraz Nawaz.

CHAPTER 12

Back in Business

Thommo confesses he has a temper, but he doesn't hold grudges. Nonetheless, to judge from the intensity of feeling at the time, it will be a long, long time before he comes to terms with some of the ups-and-downs of 1978. Back from the West Indies tour thoroughly demoralised, he threw in his lot with World Series Cricket, and then endured the alien experience of standing in court and going a few torrid rounds in the witness box.

Coming back to those 'unreal' days when he stood in the wilderness after refusing to play Test cricket and yet faced a ban on his participation in World Series:

Would you believe I had a phone call (and Frank Gardiner did too) from somebody saying he was speaking for the Australian Cricket Board, and that they'd make me Test captain if I stayed away from Packer cricket. The other part of the deal was that Steve Rixon would be out as wicketkeeper and Simmo would be dropped. I'd be captain — not that I wanted to be. Any changes that I wanted would be done, and Queensland players would be in, like John Maclean as wicketkeeper, and Gary Cosier and Geoff Dymock and Phil Carlson. Diabolical. How could you trust anybody involved in that kind of intrigue?

It was denied, of course, but it's absolutely true. I can deny whatever, but that doesn't matter. I'm only a mug.

The 'mug' was bewildered. What had happened to the champion egg-thrower of Condobolin? To the boyish-hearted fellow who used to drive round with his mate Lenny wearing imitation police caps and frightening the hell out of people? To the wild young man who sometimes got so far carried away on cockatoo hunts as to do barely forgivable things to captive birds so that their screeches would attract other cockies? Where was the laughing, teasing husband who told his wife he was about to become — for a record fee of course — the first full frontal nude in *Cleo* magazine (and was smartly and resoundingly refused permission on account of some kind of conjugal copyright on his private parts)?

He sat at the back of the courtroom reading a fishing magazine and mourning the recent death of a close friend, who was lost at sea.

Confusion and hurt turned to determination, underlined by the burning desire to win his point. 'I'm going to be busting my gut by next summer,' he told Mike Sheahan of the Melbourne *Age*. 'I want to be the best. That's what keeps me going.'

Straight after the court hearing he played for Queensland in the Gillette Cup and took six South Australian wickets for 18, winning the Man of the Match award and, in due course, a prize of two return air tickets to Fiji as Man of the Series (even though this was his one and only match). What stung him was that the medallion was engraved 'Thompson'!

Late in 1978 he took part in a tour of northern New South Wales with a team called the Cavaliers, and the lifestyle was much more his than lounging around sterile and glittering three-star hotels: many of the players camped out at night.

Then, like a sudden ray of bright sunlight zooming out of the cloudbank, it happened: the Australian Cricket Board came to an agreement with World Series Cricket and he was allowed to take part in their tour of West Indies. He was revivified:

I was actually told I was going to West Indies with World Series only about a week beforehand, which left me little time to actually step up what little training I'd been doing. But I crammed in what I could. I also had to pick up some extra needles along the way. I was pretty nervous about how I was going to go. Finally I'd reached the point where I was back on the field of play again after I don't know how many months away. It had seemed like an eternity to me. I hate watching cricket and not being able to play.

I wanted to go back onto the field and do really well, particularly after copping such a razzing in the court case. I wanted to shut everyone up. That was the main thing in my mind.

The last time I'd shared the new-ball attack with Dennis Lillee in top cricket was way back in December 1976, against Pakistan at Adelaide, when I'd crocked my shoulder. It's always been a great thrill sharing the attack with Dennis. He's such a great bowler. You tend to try a lot harder. I think even if he was dying he'd bowl himself into the ground. You say to yourself, I can't bludge along here; I've got to try harder.

In fact, as you look around the field and see all that talent there, the players that took Australia to the top in the mid 1970s, you say to yourself, I'm going to do extra well here.

When I got that first West Indian wicket, Ian Chappell came up to me and said, 'Well done, Two-up. That's your first one for Kerry.'

I thought to myself, 'Be buggered! I'm not playing for Kerry.' As far as I was concerned this was my first one for Australia again. I wasn't playing for Kerry Packer or World Series Cricket so much as the Australian side.

I think most of the fellas thought that too. We were out there trying to win for Australia. We may have been getting better pay, but we were still playing for Australia.

I think most people know me by now. I don't carry on emotionally on the field. A lot of players, when they get a wicket, do war-dances and carry on. For me, it's just part of my job. *If I don't get wickets, that's when I carry on!*

As I was saying, I trained really hard before the first game, and when Ian told me I was selected I was really proud, tickled pink. In the first one-day game, as was to be expected, I bowled all over the shop. I got a couple of wickets, but I pulled up stiff and sore the next day. Then we had to play another one-dayer. I'd learned so much from the first game that I picked up five wickets in the second. And I did it easily. Five wickets to a bowler is like scoring a hundred runs. I knew I was back then, and I was wrapped in that.

One thing concerned me though. I was stiff after each time I bowled. You can train all your life, but actually playing a match is a different thing.

My outstanding feeling as we came up to the first Supertest at Sabina Park, Kingston, was that here I was, I'd just won the Fastest Bowler in the World competition, and Viv Richards was supposed to be the 'fastest batsman in the world'! I had to make sure I did pretty well. The West Indians won easily, but I thought I bowled fairly well. When Viv came in there were plenty of runs on the board already, but somehow or other I found new, extra miles-an-hour to bowl at him, and he even said to me after a couple of overs: 'Jesus, man, you're bowling quick!' And I said, 'Yeah, I'm bowling quick at the moment, mate, but I'd better make the most of it because I'm going downhill fast!' He laughed at me.

In the room I felt I couldn't bowl the next day, because I'd really given it my all. But it was funny. I just went out there and bowled, and the stiffness just disappeared, as if somebody up there was looking after me. I really thought I'd had it. I didn't get too many wickets, but I didn't get hit around. I think most of the other guys in that game did get hit around a bit.

The thing that annoyed me about the previous tour of West Indies, with the Test team in the 1977-78 season, was that we played so feebly. I was ashamed each time we went out on the field at the batting effort we'd put up. Here I was, one year later, in a team that I considered a much better team for Australia, and I was proud to be there. I was looking forward to really giving these guys a work-out. After the first Supertest, when we lost so easily, I knew that it wouldn't happen again. It was just what our guys needed to liven them up.

On the previous tour we'd been 'rioted out' of the game in Jamaica. That wasn't a happy feeling — the first time I'd ever faced a riot. This time the crowd enjoyed the game. Perhaps our losing easily had something to do with that. They loved the cricket that both sides played, and I think Sabina Park had record gate takings.

On the whole, though, I'm a bit disenchanted about West Indies. We got through the Jamaica Supertest without a riot okay, but when we were in a winning position on the last day of the second match, at Bridgetown, Barbados, because the Press and some commentators gave their own decisions to the public without knowing what they were talking about (not being out in the middle), this egged the crowd on after quite an interesting game, and that ended up getting rioted out. That was very disappointing. We were going to win that game. That would have been very handy. It would have put us back to one-all.

In the third Supertest, at Trinidad, we were in a winning position again when Deryck Murray was run out. All right, we all get dicey decisions, but Deryck being the hometown boy, out came the bottles again. By this time it was getting a bit of a joke. We were starting to get used to this bottle caper, so we weren't going to miss out on another win. We said bugger this, and we stayed out on the field. As it turned out we overcame the crowd and we overcame West Indies, and that evened the score there.

After the Barbados match a rule was imposed to the effect that any player on either side showing dissent towards umpires would be severely reprimanded, fined, and depending on the seriousness of the dissent could even be sent home. This is how serious we were about playing our game of cricket.

In Guyana, for the fourth Supertest, it rained a lot, and we needn't have even bothered showing up at the ground on the first day. We were conned into going to the cricket ground, where they'd already let the crowd in, even though the field was saturated. So here we were, arriving at the ground, which was packed with people, who'd all paid their money, but were never going to get any refund. This was stupid, because they don't earn big wages, and it costs them a lot for the tickets.

Anyway, there we were, sitting around, and the crowd was getting restless every time the officials walked out to inspect the wicket. The umpires eventually took the bowlers out. I wasn't one of them. I was just sitting in the dressing-room. That's how much chance I thought there was of getting started. The field was too wet. Dennis Lillee, Lenny Pascoe, Greg Chappell, Colin Croft, Andy Roberts, and the 'Big Bird' Joel Garner — they all had a look. These guys weren't interested in bowling either. That's how bad the conditions were. None of us could have bowled flat-out on that wicket.

Meanwhile the crowd, who'd paid top money to watch some top cricket, had been drinking away and watching these fellas go on and off. They could sense there wasn't going to be any play, and they knew they weren't going to get their money back. It was a dynamite situation. It was only a matter of time before what was to happen actually happened. It wasn't too good.

It was a funny feeling, being in that dressing-room, which was only a timber shed, and to sit there wondering what was going to happen. I still don't know to this day what I would have done if the rioters had burst through that door. I was nearest the door. I'd closed it for the last time as the trouble boiled up, thinking to myself, 'Here we go here! It'll soon be swinging. What do I do? Go down fighting?'

Looking back on it now, you'd kill yourself laughing.

The sergeant we had in the room was unarmed — which was pretty helpful! He told us all when the bottles started coming through the windows to pick up the metal-backed chairs to guard our faces from the flying glass. Get against the wall, he said, and shield yourselves.

Some of the fellas were behind their big cricket-bags. Lenny and myself were near the doorway still, and the sergeant was next to me. All of a sudden some pretty big objects come sailing through the windows, and he's bolted. He's as scared as anyone, and he jumps down next to me, and next thing he's trying to rip my chair off me! Pulling away like hell, trying to protect himself. I turned round to him and said, 'Hey, go and get your own bloody chair.' And I ripped it back off him.

It was unbelievable. Here was this police sergeant, supposed to be looking after us, and he's ripping my shield away from me!

There were a few other blokes who were as pale as ghosts, and I didn't blame them. One of the guys said that if we'd had to make a run for it he would have got about two yards because his legs would have collapsed from under him. Max Walker didn't help matters by clicking his camera madly in all directions, which might have put a few fellas' courage into some doubt! But we won't go into that.

When it had all subsided, and everyone was safe, there was the sergeant and his offsiders lashing into our grog in the fridge! They were having a ball with the chicken and the beer.

About ten minutes later, when the blokes had had about three beers each and got their courage back, they all started to get a bit chirpy then.

The only problem left was getting away from the ground. We left by a secret exit over the other side, tricking the people who hung around in bunches all the way back to the hotel apparently, waiting to pelt the bus with some more objects. We went a different route, and we had an escort van.

But what does our bus-driver do? On the way back to the hotel he overtakes the armed escort! We're left out on our own, and the guys are screaming at him 'Get back, you bloody idiot! You've left the escort behind us now, you goose!' It was a circus.

As you can imagine, when we got back to the hotel that night and got safely within the walls there, there was some booze drunk. People were glad to be alive.

We went back the next day, showing the crowd that we were prepared to play cricket for them, despite the riot. I remember our manager on the previous tour, Fred Bennett, a man I respect very much, and who'd been through a few riots in his day, saying during a team meeting when we were discussing whether to continue with the game after that particular disturbance, that the crowd weren't going to overrun us. We were going back there to show them.

I'll give the West Indian crowd this much: they're knowledgable and unbelievably keen. I think this is why they're so excitable. On the whole they're probably one of the best crowds to play in front of.

Michael Holding had a good series. He bowled pretty steadily, very fast at times, generally using his head. Colin Croft bowled pretty well, but Andy Roberts bowled within himself. He bowled well, but I've seen him quicker. One of the best innings was Clive Lloyd's 197 at Kingston. It took me back to Roy Fredericks' 169 against Australia in 1975 at Perth. There were some beautiful strokes in it. Andy Roberts showed the world that he's no mug with the bat either with 89 in this Sabina Park game.

Roy Fredericks was consistent throughout the tour. He was a thorn in our side, and we were always glad to see him go. He's one guy who can really boost the run rate along. Lawrence Rowe was unfortunate in the first Supertest to be hit a pretty bad blow from Dennis Lillee. Perhaps he was fortunate — to get off with such a slight injury. It looked really bad at the time. That put him out for a time, but he came back with a century in the final game, at St John's.

For us, Greg Chappell was back to his best form of old, and one of the biggest thrills was seeing Rod Marsh make a hundred in the fifth Supertest, when we went in a second time over 200 runs behind, and finished over 200 runs ahead with a few wickets in hand.

David Hookes was disappointing. He lacked a lot of thought in what he was doing, I thought. He didn't do his homework properly in what he was doing wrong. I think he'll look at that in the future though.

We were a bit short of batsmen, as it turned out. Rick McCosker got a broken thumb first up, and Trevor Chappell got a cut jaw. So we were behind the eight ball, and I thought we did pretty well to end up all square in the Supertests.

One of the stars to emerge was a batsman we all know has lots of ability, and that's Martin Kent. Batting at number three, one of the most responsible spots, he batted absolutely beautifully, and West Indies were always very pleased to get him out cheaply.

The grounds in West Indies seemed in better condition than they were the year before — a bit softer. Considering that they don't have much to work on, they prepared some good pitches. The one at Port of Spain, Trinidad, probably needs replacing. It's a terrible sort of wicket to play any sort of entertaining cricket on.

The weather was unbelievable. It rained on virtually every day of the tour. But our team spirit was high, and that got us by. Quite a contrast to the previous year.

After losing the first Supertest, we really wanted the big effort, and I remember distinctly how we relaxed before the team meeting in Barbados. I'd organised a fishing trip for a few of the guys and some of the camera crew, out with Richard Edwards, the former West Indies fast bowler. I thought it looked a bit rough out there, as Lenny and I had been going down the beach for a surf each day. It had gradually been getting rougher and rougher. I think some of the blokes expected to come back with a 1000 lb marlin or something, but they came back at seven o'clock that evening without a thing! A few of them were sick, and one of the camera crew had spent most of the day down below.

We were due to have a fish barbecue that night, and I'd told them that whatever they caught, I'd cook it for them. But for safety's sake I went down to the local fish markets with Lenny and bought some fish just in case. I somehow didn't think they'd get too many. My cooking went down really well, and helped the team spirit! The team meeting led to a big effort from the boys, and on the whole we played really well from then on.

I'd like to say something about Ian Chappell as a captain at this point. 'Bertie's' been the best captain in the world for some time as far as I'm concerned. I hadn't played under him for several years before this tour of West Indies, but he hadn't lost any of his old spark. He's probably improved, in fact. He's always got the players' admiration, and you try that much harder for him. If he tells you something you know it's right. He's a pretty shrewd customer and you respect how much he tries himself.

An example of how 'Bertie' operates was in Barbados. Lenny Pascoe hadn't played up to that point. As everyone knows, Lenny's a great friend of mine, and we'd been going to the beach. I needed a rest after the initial effort after playing in every game in Jamaica, and Lenny wasn't happy at all, and decided he needed a rest as well. 'Bertie' decided, though, that we needed the extra pace bowler to fix these West Indian blokes up, and Lenny was going to be it. But Lenny had decided he wasn't going to be it. He was going to be down the beach with me.

We happened to be going downstairs in the hotel this day, and the bus was just leaving for a non-compulsory practice session. Greg Chappell and myself had decided to go to the beach. So Lenny said, 'Bugger this, I'm not going to the practice. I'm going down the beach as well.'

He's halfway down the stairs when he spots the bus. He says, 'Hey, they haven't gone yet. I'd better not go out yet.'

Then he spots Ian Chappell over the road, so he runs round the back of the hotel like a little kid, and says 'Tell him you don't know where I am!' So I kept walking. And 'Bertie' comes running up to me and says 'Have you seen your big mate?'

I said, 'Ah, well, he was just upstairs with me, as a matter of fact. But he left. I don't know where he is.'

I kept walking back to the hotel, and 'Bertie's' gone back looking for Lenny. Lenny's still hiding in the bushes behind the hotel. Diabolical when you think about it!

Anyway, the bus has left, but Ian said to me, 'If you see Lenny tell him to get his arse to practice. I want him there to bowl.'

With the bus gone, Lenny comes out of the bushes, but Greg Chappell says to him, 'Where you been?' 'Over there. Why?' says Lenny. 'Well,' says Greg, 'Ian says you'd better get to the practice. Get in a cab and get over there.'

You can imagine Lenny by now. He was spewing. 'Non-compulsory practice,' he growls. 'I'm not going there.'

Off he went, though. And he had to pay for the taxi himself. When he gets there he starts abusing everyone. He's like a bear with a bee in his bonnet. And he bowled hand-grenades at the batsmen. Bounced hell out of them; especially Ian Chappell and Rod Marsh. Picked up the ball as soon as Ian came into the net, and let him have it.

It was just what Ian wanted him to do. It gave him the practice against bouncers that he dearly wanted. Dennis and myself hadn't been bouncing anyone at the nets. We'd been looking after ourselves for the matches. But here's Lenny, not quite understanding what he was doing, helping the captain — and himself as well. He bowled really well in the Supertest. And 'Bertie' made runs in both digs too.

That's the sort of bloke Ian Chappell is.

To put a check on players' behaviour on the tour, fines were put on for swearing, for not being punctual, and for virtually anything that was degrading for the Australian image. These were imposed by a committee selected by the players themselves. Most of the guys on the tour received a fine of some sort of other, and some of them paid up numerous fines!

By the end of the tour I dearly wanted to get home. I'd missed my wife Cheryl during the couple of months we'd been away. But the first thing I wanted was a decent feed, because West Indian food does not suit my diet at all. I remember when we arrived in San Francisco en route for home that we went down to Fisherman's Wharf the very next morning and bought crabs, prawns, bread — picture it: Lenny and myself roaming the streets with that little lot at six in the morning! We sat down on an old log near the wharf and filled ourselves. Soon afterwards we had a huge lunch. I just sat there and thought about what I'd come from and what I was going back to, and I just couldn't *wait*.

As it was, I flew home early, on my own. If that plane could have flown any faster I'd have helped it.

At last, on May 30, it was announced that the 'war' between the Australian Cricket Board and Kerry Packer's World Series Cricket was over. A peace formula had been worked out after two years of turmoil, ill-feeling and lost revenue.

Just as revolutions of this kind are never bloodless or never soft on the ear, so no armistice can be instantaneous in its appeal to all parties concerned. As the 1979-80 season approached there was talk of World Series players fearing victimisation — even though the threat of discrimination was thought to have been dealt with satisfactorily to the principals in the final document. There was talk also of the World Series players 'going after' those who had neither joined nor approved of them, and of them helping each other during the Sheffield Shield matches preceding the big matches against England and West Indies — while Kim Hughes and his young team were in India.

At least one cricketer was overjoyed at the truce — even if he had not yet completely purged his mind of unforgiving thoughts:

When news of the compromise between World Series Cricket and the Australian Board came through, I was glad. The major thing I wanted — as did all the other guys — was for Australian cricket to be number one again. Despite what money comes into professional cricket, I think I can speak also for the rest of the players: Australia comes first.

The biggest pleasure and the biggest laugh I got at the announcement was the sight of the photo of Bob Parish, the ACB chairman, with his arm around Lynton Taylor, the WSC managing director, after Mr Parish had heaped so much muck on me in the court case, and after he'd bagged World Series so much. Now here he was, with his arm around a WSC official, saying 'I'm glad we're together' sort of thing. I just had to laugh.

Now I've got something fresh to aim for. I think a lot of the younger players who got Australian Test places while the World Series players were absent will have to move over. I think they've had a nice run, and they've had international experience, which they wouldn't have got otherwise. Now they'll have to wait in the wings. The experience they've had will benefit them in the long run.

I earned my green cap the hard way, as most of the other guys did, and I'm not about to give it up easily. The competition now is going to be fierce and fast. Lenny Pascoe said just the other day that he's going to knock off Hoggy. I can tell you this: I'm going to make it hot for all these blokes. I'm going to have a real big year in 1979-80.

I'm sure the Australian selectors really will go for the best side. The public naturally want to see it. There will probably be a few worries among the administrators. But it's like I've said all along, administration worries and all that caper, that's not my bag. What I do best is play cricket, and that's all I worry about. I'll get out in the middle there and I can assure you, I'll be trying my best.

Ian Chappell's the guy who can put Australia back as number one. I'm not sure at this moment whether he'll be available. But he's the man. He deserves the chance, too. He's sacrificed a lot, and copped a lot of muck. I couldn't think of anything better than to give him the Australian Test captaincy, the best team, and for us to beat everyone — a clean sweep.

As for Queensland, the State has got to be captained by Greg Chappell. There's nobody else you'd even look at, or who even comes within a whisker of his ability. I'm certainly looking forward to playing for Queensland again. I recently received a letter saying I'd been selected in the pre-season practice squad, and I was pleased about that. I'm looking forward to the Sheffield Shield season as much as anything.

As I said earlier, when I run out of goals in my sporting life then that's the day to give away big-time cricket and think about something else. But I've still got a bit to prove. I've played with and against some great players, and learned to respect some of the greats from just earlier than my time, blokes like Freddie Trueman and Wes Hall and Garry Sobers.

Most of the Australian Test cricketers of old are pretty good blokes too. You have to make allowances sometimes. Everyone talks about *their day*. I'll probably get old too, and say 'Imagine how we had to bowl against these blokes in our day' in about twenty-five years' time!

Once I'm finished, that'll be it. I don't see myself as a writer or commentator. I can't see myself hanging around. I like the bush and the ocean too much. I like living as it comes. I couldn't even tell you what I'm doing tomorrow most of the time. That's the way I like living. To wake up and look in the diary and say I've got to do this or that today — I'd cut my throat if I had to live that way. Maybe I'm not as bad as Denis Compton, who apparently tuned into his car radio many years ago and heard he was about to come out of the pavilion and go out to bat in a Test match. He still had a couple of miles to drive! I like old Compo. We went to a couple of good parties in 1975. He's real easy-going, does his own thing. He's a good bloke.

The amount of cut-throat business that goes on around the place makes me sick. I like basic things: for people to be honest with you and you be honest with them. People weren't honest with me a lot in the past year or so. That's where I came undone.

Looking into the future, I love cricket. I missed the action when I was banned during 1978-79. I missed playing. I missed being with the blokes afterwards. It's always been my life. I've played since I was nine. I know I'll have to face it eventually, that I've got nothing much left to offer. But I don't want to think about that at the moment. As each year comes I don't think I get any slower. I do a bit of work to keep me there. But I must lose my pace sometime. That's when I'll give it away, unless I bowl medium-pace.

Final observation from co-author: Thommo bowling medium-pace! That's as unthinkable as Phar Lap pulling a plough or Ned Kelly playing with a popgun.

Jeff Thomson in Figures

Statistics by Andrew Thomas

TEST MATCHES FOR AUSTRALIA

Bowling

	Balls	Maid.	Runs	Wick.	Aver.	Best Fig.	5 wkts/ inns	Catch.
1972-73 v Pakistan	152	1	110	0	—	—	0	0
1974-75 v England	1401	34	592	33	17.94	6/46	2	3
1975 v England	1051	56	457	16	28.56	5/38	1	3
1975-76 v West Indies	1205	15	831	29	28.66	6/50	2	3
1976-77 v Pakistan	69	2	34	2	17.00	2/34	0	0
1977 v England	1205	44	583	23	25.35	4/41	0	0
1977-78 v India	1167	21	516	22	23.45	4/76	0	2
1978 v West Indies	908	25	577	20	28.85	6/77	1	2
	7158	198	3700	145	25.52	6/46	6	13

SUMMARY

	Balls	Maid.	Runs	Wick.	Aver.	Best Fig.	5 wkts/ inns	Catch.
v Pakistan	221	3	144	2	72.00	2/34	0	0
v England	3657	134	1632	72	22.67	6/46	3	6
v West Indies	2113	40	1408	49	28.73	6/50	3	5
v India	1167	21	516	22	23.45	4/76	0	2
	7158	198	3700	145	25.52	6/46	6	13

Batting

	M	I	N.O.	H.S.	Runs	Av.
1972-73 v Pakistan	1	1	1	19*	19	—
1974-75 v England	5	5	2	24*	65	21.67
1975 v England	4	4	0	49	82	20.50
1975-76 v West Indies	6	7	0	44	63	9.00
1976-77 v Pakistan	1	0	0	—	0	—
1977 v England	5	8	1	21	59	8.43
1977-78 v India	5	10	3	41*	101	14.43
1978 v West Indies	5	8	0	12	35	4.38
	32	43	7	49	424	11.78

SUMMARY

	M	I	N.O.	H.S.	Runs	Av.
v Pakistan	2	1	1	19*	19	—
v England	14	17	3	49	206	14.71
v West Indies	11	15	0	44	98	6.53
v India	5	10	3	41*	101	14.43
	32	43	7	49	424	11.78

ALL FIRST-CLASS MATCHES

Bowling

	Balls	Maid.	Runs	Wick.	Aver.	Best Fig.	5 wkts/ inns	Catch.
1972-73	1280	21	649	18	36.06	4/65	0	2
1973-74	245	5	125	9	13.89	7/85	1	0
1974-75	2711	61	1201	62	19.37	6/17	3	8
1975 in England	2029	88	1059	34	31.15	5/38	1	5
1975-76	2644	39	1473	62	23.76	6/47	4	6
1976-77	935	25	378	27	14.00	7/33	3	0
1977 in England	2312	84	1207	43	28.07	4/41	0	3
1977-78	2506	33	1246	57	21.86	5/70	3	3
1978 in West Indies	1118	34	679	24	28.29	6/77	1	3
	15780	390	8017	336	23.86	7/33	16	30

Batting

	M	I	N.O.	H.S.	Runs	Av.
1972-73	7	8	4	30*	82	20.50
1973-74	1	2	2	2*	2	—
1974-75	12	15	3	61	161	13.42
1975 in England	10	10	4	49	186	31.00
1975-76	14	17	1	44.	175	10.94
1976-77	5	5	0	32	65	13.00
1977 in England	16	17	1	25	130	8.13
1977-78	11	18	6	41*	183	15.25
1978 in West Indies	8	12	3	19*	58	6.44
	84	104	24	61	1042	13.03

Index